Advance Praise for *Clash of the Generations*

Leaders are still struggling to motivate Millennials in the workplace—and now Generation Z is on the doorstep. Grubb offers concrete suggestions on how to engage four generations that each have very different expectations of their managers and organizations. If you are only going to read, one management book this year—this is the one. It is a joy to read, with lively writing and practical advice.

Timothy T. Baldwin, Professor and Chair
Department of Management and Entrepreneurship
Indiana University Kelley School of Business

Val Grubb has succinctly and accurately captured the new workplace reality in a voice that is easy to read. Her practical advice for thriving in and building a generationally diverse organization is spot on. I like books that present real-world solutions, but I love books that ask the right questions! I wish I had coauthored it!

Chip Espinoza, PhD
Author, *Managing the Millennials:*
Discover the Core Competencies of Managing Today's Workforce

From the first page, *Clash of the Generations* hits you with staggering statistics and hard facts. Grubb has written a masterful book that captures the essence of generational conflict and provides savvy solutions. *Clash of the Generations* is not a life preserver but a speedboat to multigenerational success.

Meagan Johnson, Generational Humorist
Author, *Generations, Inc.: From Boomers to Linksters—*
Managing the Friction Between Generations at Work

Grubb's many years of leading and managing generationally diverse teams and consulting to best-in-class companies make *Clash of the Generations* a compelling look into how the workforce is changing—and changing fast. Anyone passionate about developing his or her leadership skills and learning to navigate—and get the best of—rapidly diversifying workforces will find her strategies not only cutting edge, but immediately practical. A must-read for leaders at all levels!

Jennifer Brown, President and CEO
Jennifer Brown Consulting
Author, *Inclusion: Diversity, the New Workplace & the*
Will to Change

CLASH

OF THE

GENERATIONS

CLASH

OF THE

GENERATIONS

MANAGING THE NEW
WORKPLACE REALITY

VALERIE M. GRUBB

This book is printed on acid-free paper. ∞

Copyright © 2017 by Valerie M. Grubb. All rights reserved

Published by John Wiley & Sons, Inc., Hoboken, New Jersey
Published simultaneously in Canada

For general information about our other products and services, please contact our Customer Care
Department within the United States at (800) 762-2974, outside the United States at (317) 572-3993 or fax
(317) 572-4002.

Wiley publishes in a variety of print and electronic formats and by print-on-demand. Some material
included with standard print versions of this book may not be included in e-books or in print-on-demand. If
this book refers to media such as a CD or DVD that is not included in the version you purchased, you may
download this material at http://booksupport.wiley.com. For more information about Wiley products, visit
www.wiley.com.

Library of Congress Cataloging-in-Publication Data

Names: Grubb, Valerie M., author.
Title: Clash of the generations : managing the new workplace reality /
   Valerie M. Grubb.
Description: Hoboken : Wiley, 2016. | Includes bibliographical references and
   index.
Identifiers: LCCN 2016030971| ISBN 9781119212348 (hardback) |
   ISBN 9781119212461 (Adobe PDF) | ISBN 9781119212478 (epub)
Subjects: LCSH: Diversity in the workplace—Management. | Conflict of
   generations in the workplace—Management. | Intergenerational relations. |
   Older people—Employment. | Youth—Employment. | BISAC: BUSINESS &
   ECONOMICS / Human Resources & Personnel Management.
Classification: LCC HF5549.5.C75 G78 2016 | DDC 331.3–dc23 LC record available at
   https://lccn.loc.gov/2016030971

Cover design: Wiley

Printed in the United States of America

10 9 8 7 6 5 4 3 2 1

For my father, Byron E. Grubb,
who taught me to respect everyone, regardless of his or her rank or status.
You are missed.

CONTENTS

PREFACE

By 2020, 25 percent of the labor force will be over the age of 55—and they're not retiring any time soon. The result? A clash of cultures that requires a new management approach.

In recent years there's been a lot of talk about generation-related issues in the workplace—especially the impending en masse retirement of the Baby Boomers. Senior leaders and HR executives were warned to prepare for the knowledge exodus that would take place when the Baby Boomers retired in droves and to prepare to manage the generations (in particular, the Millennials) that would replace them.

The reality, however, is that Boomers *haven't* been retiring in the numbers originally expected. In fact, the average retirement age has steadily been creeping up (it's now at 61), and recent statistics indicate that this number will continue to increase. A recent Gallup Poll found that 24 percent of Baby Boomers are waiting until age 65 to retire, and 49 percent are planning to hold off until 66 or older. In addition, researchers at the Stanford Center on Longevity estimate that by 2020, 25 percent of the labor force will be 55 and over—a sharp jump from 13 percent in 2000. In the near future, we may even see people working to 100 (and beyond!).

Because Baby Boomers are prolonging their time in the workplace, the old business model of "the mature retire to make way for the new" no longer applies. Instead of the previous cycle of succeeding generations, companies now find themselves with workforces that cover a wider range of ages than ever before. Senior leaders, managers, and HR professionals must manage a blended workforce spanning four generations that vary wildly in their work ethics, ideas about work-life balance, and long-term career goals, among other concerns.

Managing employees is a challenging endeavor under any circumstances— and it's even more difficult in the midst of generational culture clash. Drawing on my experiences over more than two decades of managing thousands of employees and on interviews with representatives of several companies with age-diverse workforces, this book details proven strategies that managers and senior leaders can employ to motivate and engage even their most challenging direct reports.

ACKNOWLEDGMENTS

This book is the result of many lessons learned over the years from managing thousands of employees—from my first Plant 8 maintenance crew at Allison Gas Turbine in 1989, to those who work for me now at my own consulting company, and everyone in between. Thank you for teaching me what it means to be a good manager. This journey has been a blast, and no matter where you are now in your lives and careers, I wish you all the best.

I would also like to thank my dear friend Marsha Jane Brofka-Berends, who continues to amaze me with her editorial prowess. I thought this book, a huge and challenging undertaking, would send her running, but fortunately it didn't (and she's already committed to working on my next one!). I am also grateful to Sarah Barasch for her stellar research, in which she left no stone unturned. We worked together at Oxygen years ago, and it's been wonderful to reconnect with her through this project. My thanks also go out to Jenna Rose Robbins for her invaluable research and editorial contributions to this work.

Many thanks to Jeanenne Ray, my editor at John Wiley & Sons, for recognizing the importance of this topic. Thanks, too, to Heather Brosius for answering all my questions along the way. It's been a pleasure working with both of you.

Finally, I would be remiss if I didn't thank my mom, Dorothy Grubb, and my brother, Eric Grubb, for putting up with me when I write. I can be a bear, but you love me anyway—and for that I am forever grateful. Thank you! I love you both dearly as well.

Chapter 1

THE NEW WORKPLACE REALITY

Clinging to the past is the problem. Embracing change is the solution.
—Gloria Steinem, *Moving Beyond Words*[1]

S ince the first major round of corporate downsizing in the 1980s, the longtime traditional employment trajectory has been in flux. Gone are the days when people entered the workforce as young adults, worked until their mid-50s or so, and then sailed off into retirement while younger generations took their place. Instead, the average retirement age has steadily been creeping up in recent decades as older employees—in particular, the Baby Boomers—stay in the workforce either by choice or by necessity. Medical and technological advances mean we're living much longer than previous generations. But the financial instability caused by the 2008 recession has taken a massive toll on retirement plans, requiring many older employees to remain in the workforce longer. Boomers aren't continuing to work only because they *have* to, though: many of them continue to work because they *want* to, thanks in part to the growing availability of office jobs that people can continue to do regardless of age. In addition, many Boomers just enjoy the camaraderie and social connectivity of the workplace. And Boomers often have a lot of pride in their career—a sentiment that can make them inclined to stay in the workplace longer.[2]

In recent years, though, a new generation has become the largest group in the labor market: the Millennials. In early 2015, a Pew Research Center study found that for the first time the workplace included more Millennials (nearly 54 million) than Baby Boomers (nearly 53 million) or members of Generation X (just under 45 million).[3] With so many younger employees joining the workforce, one might assume that the median age of US workers was decreasing. Surprisingly, that is *not* the case.

According to the Bureau of Labor Statistics (BLS) at the US Department of Labor, in 2004 the median working age was 40.3 years but in 2014 it had climbed to 41.9 years—and by 2024 it is expected to hit 42.4 years.[4] Interestingly, although the Millennial numbers are far greater than the current figures of earlier generations, the BLS report states that "the average annual growth rate of the 55-years-and-older group [is] projected to be 1.8 percent, more than three times the rate of growth of the overall labor force," adding that "the group's share of the labor force is anticipated to increase from 21.7 percent in 2014 to nearly 25 percent in 2024."[5] These projections indicate that not only will Baby Boomers continue to work alongside their current Generation X and Millennial colleagues, but that they will still be around when Generation Z join the workforce.

That is potentially good news for companies experiencing a shortage of workers, particularly in skilled trades. But when three or even four generations are sharing the office, getting everyone to work together toward a common goal becomes even

3

more challenging. Senior leaders, managers, and HR professionals need to be prepared to manage a workforce spanning multiple generations with wildly different ideas about work ethic, work-life balance, and long-term career goals, among many other issues. Each age cohort brings its own expectations, goals, motivations, and experiences into the office every day, and company leaders, managers, and human resources executives who want to succeed must understand those differences in order to minimize conflict and create a productive workplace.

THE CHANGING NATURE OF LEADERSHIP

As the Loretta Lynn song says, "We've come a long way, baby." Over the past half century or so, workplace practices and expectations have changed dramatically—and for the better. When the first Baby Boomers entered the workforce, they were taught that leaders give orders, ensure that the orders are followed, and deal with employees who don't comply. The dictatorial leader is rapidly disappearing from today's workplace, though, having been replaced by leaders who are expected to build partnerships both inside and outside the organization—a shift in leadership styles that recognizes that coalition building can be more effective for companies than rigid control. Does this shift mean that a manager can't make decisions unless all of his or her direct reports agree with them? Of course not. It *does* mean, though, that employees of any age will expect to have input on decisions that affect them, and that the lack of such input will significantly diminish their commitment to accomplishing the company's goals.

The changing expectations for company leaders are also being shaped by the fact that employees of all ages lack trust in corporate America. During the 1980s, Baby Boomers and Generation X lost that trust during the heyday of building shareholder value through layoffs, when even healthy companies joined the downsizing movement in order to increase their market shares. Millennials, too, aren't exhibiting great faith in the business world today, and if these trends continue, this lack of trust is likely to still be around when Generation Z begins to enter the workforce. Regardless of the decade or the generation, though, this lack of trust—and the resulting lack of strong loyalty to a company—can affect *everyone* negatively, particularly when employees favor pursuing career advancement elsewhere over staying with their current organizations. In order to prevent that exodus, managers need to figure out how to adapt to changing expectations about employee loyalty.

The changing demographic within the United States (nay, the *world*) is another cultural shift that will require leaders to rethink not just their leadership styles but their entire business plans, because the employee base isn't the only population that's changing: customers and suppliers are changing as well. Over the next few decades, the United States will become an older and more ethnically diverse country. For example, according to the US Census Bureau, over the next few decades, nonwhite ethnic groups will increase in number dramatically, and by 2042 no single ethnic group will be the majority. The Hispanic population will be the leaders of this demographic shift, with its size "more than [doubling], from 53.3 million in 2012 to 128.8 million in 2060."[6] Also expected to double in size by 2060 is the population age 65 and older, which will grow from 43.1 million to 92.0 million.

Many would argue that corporate leadership has had to deal with managing change for at least the past decade or so. As Ad J. Scheepbouwer (then-CEO of Royal KPN) pointed out in IBM's 2008 survey of 1,000 CEOs, "We have seen more change in the last 10 years than in the previous 90."[7] Technological advances drove most of that change and continue to do so, with Scheepbouwer's words still applicable nearly a decade after he uttered them. In spite of widespread awareness of such change, many companies' management practices have failed to respond to the new workplace reality.

Shocking but true: even though the first Millennials joined the workplace roughly 10 years ago, many companies *still* struggle to figure out how to cope with the Millennials in their midst. And with the first members of Generation Z poised to enter the workforce full time in just a few short years and other changing workplace demographics, the stage is set for disaster for those companies still lagging in their management practices. Even with these realities staring them in the face, though, many companies *still* resist change. Why? Because change is hard—even when (and sometimes especially if) it's absolutely necessary. But market-leading organizations recognize the importance of change and achieve success in part because of their ability to adapt rapidly to the changing needs of their customers and clients. Those companies embrace change because doing so lets them create new opportunities *ahead* of their competitors.

Enacting change at your organization means updating your leadership tactics, which in turn means letting go of old habits and instead thinking about motivation and engagement in a new light—a task that isn't easy to accomplish in even the most relaxed and low-stakes situations, let alone when engaging in something as difficult (and somewhat esoteric) as managing employees. Unfortunately, managing employees is even more complicated by the fact that according to Gallup only "one in 10 people possess the inherent talent to manage"—and companies fail to pick good managers a staggering 82 percent of the time.[8] When this is combined with the added challenge of having four generations in the workplace, the odds increase that companies will experience high turnover or low employee engagement (both of which can hugely affect an organization's bottom line)—and managing becomes a lot more complicated.

THE CHANGING ROLE OF THE MANAGER

Managing employees has always been tough for newbie and veteran managers alike. If you're like most managers, you didn't start your career in management but got promoted to a supervisory role based on your superior contributions as an employee. Consequently, you may find yourself with direct reports who may or may not be at your skill level (and may even be more skilled than you). As a manager, you're expected to motivate them to complete their tasks on time and to your quality specifications, but you have to be careful that this motivation doesn't cross the line into micromanagement. Easy, right? Not quite.

Getting work done through the efforts of others is incredibly different—and far more challenging—than doing it yourself, and few new managers are fully prepared for that shift when they're promoted. And help in dealing with that shift is in short supply: in a 2011 CareerBuilder survey, for example, nearly 60 percent of respondents said they "didn't receive any management training."[9] When that lack of training meets the various (and sometimes conflicting) expectations of employees in a multigenerational workplace, the result is a potent mix of management challenges! Baby Boomers want respect for their experience, Generation Xers want autonomy and money, and Millennials want a team environment coupled with more frequent recognition. Even when the generations agree on certain issues (such as a shared desire to increase work-life balance through more flexible work schedules), addressing them can still present plenty of challenges for managers.[10]

Finding ways to accommodate employees' needs in order to motivate and engage them (and actually accomplish the work for which their managers are ultimately responsible!) has become a critical part of management in recent years—and one that not only differs greatly from management's role in the past but a task that can be tough to accomplish, particularly in companies without policies that support their employees' needs.

As you progress on your own management journey (whether you're just starting on this path or have been on it for a while and seek to expand your existing skills), keep in mind that being an effective manager in the new workplace will require much more adaptation from you than from your employees. Throughout my 20 years in management, I've found that the challenge of managing and motivating others doesn't diminish over time. Even as you become more experienced, typical company turnover as well as changing career trajectories mean that you're constantly dealing with new people. Some of your reports will be promoted outside your group, be reassigned to other departments, or move to other organizations, for example—or perhaps *you* will be the one who is promoted, is reassigned, or changes organizations. Every time you think you've put together a cohesive team, the group will change (either by addition or by subtraction), and you'll have to start the process anew.

Even though it's important to recognize that each generation has different expectations, it's equally important to recognize the dangers of stereotyping someone based on his or her age. When managing individuals, always keep in mind that they have unique needs that are determined by their particular life circumstances and personal goals. So even as you consider how generational influences may manifest in the office, remember that successfully managing *anyone* to achieve his or her best will require you to treat the person primarily as an individual and not exclusively as part of a generational cohort.

For example, during my eight-year tenure with Oxygen Media, I managed a total of 55 employees who were spread across various departments and whose ages spanned 40 years. It would have been easy for me to categorize them based on their ages (and, based on those, my assumptions about their needs). In practice, though, I found that each individual sought different kinds of fulfillment in his or her work. Each employee also had different expectations of me as the manager, and everyone needed me to motivate him or her in different ways. For example, one of my direct reports needed to be left alone for the first hour of the day so she could ascertain her priorities—and give time for her espresso to kick in—whereas another preferred to start his work day with a brief meeting with me. One of my main responsibilities as a manager was to figure out what each *individual* needed to do his or her job well and then do my best to provide it.

In fact, over the course of my entire work life, I've found that individual motivation is always the main influence on employee behavior. This has been true right from the beginning, when I first started my career as an engineer at Allison Gas Turbine, an aircraft engine manufacturing facility in Indianapolis. The ages of the 52-member all-male maintenance crew I managed ranged from 15 years older than me to 44 years older than me. The six-decade age span was a bit daunting at first, but I soon realized that in spite of the vast age differences, we all had *the work* in common, and the key was to understand how each *individual* sought fulfillment in that work. Some employees needed my approval before proceeding on even the most mundane tasks, for example, and others preferred not to see me at all until the job was done. Some employees fought for overtime, and others avoided it like the plague. Each man cared about different things and held different expectations of me.

At first I thought I was going to lose my mind trying to navigate all the different personalities! Eventually this job—my first management assignment—taught me a very valuable lesson that I've carried with me ever since: *figuring out what makes each person perform at his or her best is one of the most satisfying experiences a manager can have in corporate America.*

When managing others, you are directly responsible for helping each person perform better, and succeeding at that task can give you a pretty powerful and wonderful feeling. So as you contemplate what it takes to manage and lead others, keep in mind that you'll need to adapt your style to meet the individual needs of your employees. And if you're older than—or younger than—your employees, keep your eye on the goal (helping them do their best work) and not on your age differences.

If you're a Millennial who's in a management position, for example, not knowing how to ask someone older than you to do something is no excuse for bypassing or ignoring senior employees who possess information critical to the company. By that same token, if you're an older manager, you need to recognize that Millennials are essential to the future growth and *very existence* of every company and that being able to keep them engaged and excited to work with you is of paramount importance. By stepping up your management game, you'll have a better shot at keeping the brightest and best employees—whatever their ages—working for you.

THE CHANGING ROLE OF HR

Managing in the new workplace reality is hard on everyone but especially for those in HR who are charged with overseeing a company's human capital programs. During the recent recession, companies had the upper hand when it came to talent: because there were more people looking for jobs than there were available jobs, employees were extremely wary of leaving their positions. With the improvement of the economy, however, the pendulum has swung the other way, and in the post-recession years organizations are having to work harder than ever to recruit top performers. Companies are currently experiencing the HR version of real estate's buyer's market: there are too many jobs and not enough people to fill them. Consequently, current and prospective employees can be a lot pickier about what positions they fill.

For example, over the past decade, Millennials have entered the workforce to find it already a very crowded place, full not only of Generation X employees but also of older workers who haven't been retiring in the numbers that were expected (and highly discussed) around the turn of the millennium. Complicating matters further is the fact that many Millennials expect to love their jobs and want more than just a paycheck: they want missions that they can support and companies that are interested in their personal growth. For these reasons, more so than any other generation, Millennials are far more likely to quit a job that they don't like (whereas Generation Xers and Baby Boomers are a little more patient about waiting for a promotion or more opportunities). Millennials aren't the only ones being choosy, though. As any HR executive can tell you, when Generation X or Baby Boomer employees find that their needs aren't being met, they, too, will look for other opportunities.

Adding to the challenges facing the HR executive are the company leaders who do not fully embrace the policies and practices that support the expectations of today's workforce. Corporate leaders love to tout inclusion and diversity as company priorities, but in many instances their efforts amount to little more than merely checking a box and don't actually have an effect on corporate culture. If diversity and inclusion are treated as "nice to have" initiatives (and not as high-priority business imperatives), they can receive mixed support from up high—and there's only so much HR can accomplish in an organization without strong support from senior management. If your company fits this description, it's important for you to demonstrate the bottom-line value of diversity and inclusion *before* trying to make any changes. If the top executives don't see that value, you'll find it difficult to update existing programs or roll out new ones designed to engage employees of all ages.

What do most senior management teams care about? The bottom line. Focusing on that is the key to persuading your executives to embrace the business case for diversity. A great place to start is by analyzing your customer base (that's right, your *customer* base) first—even before looking at your employee base. Discussions about sales will certainly get your CEO's attention. So involve the senior sales executives and review the generational demographics of your current clients or customers. Does your workforce reflect the generational makeup of your customer base? Is the company missing any opportunities by not servicing all age levels with its product? If so, how can the organization best reach those overlooked age groups?

Next, review projected growth for your company, both in terms of volume and in terms of product offerings. Discuss the following questions:

- How does the projected growth compare to the projected makeup of your employee base in the future? Are the two proportionately equal?
- Will the generational makeup of your employee base 5 or 10 years from now reflect your customer base at that time?
- Does your product age with your customers, or will your customers look to a competitor as they (and your existing product) grow older? How can you keep your customers coming back to you and buying more of your product instead of moving to your competitors?

Mirroring your employee base on your customer base can help ensure that your products stay relevant to your customers as they age. As your older employees find their own needs changing, they'll know how to adapt your products to meet the needs of your similarly aged customers. Having diverse ages in the workplace can also help reduce the groupthink that can dominate employee populations that are homogeneous in age and background (the "like hires like" phenomenon), thus providing the broadest range of ideas possible for your products and services. Pay attention to whether the local population is aging (or trending younger), and how that shift might affect both your sales numbers and your recruiting and retention efforts. The savviest organizations are radically modifying their business practices *now* in order to prepare for future changes in their employee base and (perhaps more importantly) in their customer and client bases as well.

One reality that's having a huge impact on the bottom line is the difficulty many companies are having filling open positions with people who have the particular skills needed to do those jobs. The so-called skills gap continues to grow each year, making hiring increasingly difficult and bringing challenges to retention as well. If your most experienced employees leave your company, does that help or hurt its skills gap? What is the sweet spot where your company has sufficient employees of all ages with enough diverse skill sets (including both experience and newer skills) to mitigate—or even eliminate—the skills gap?

If bringing in younger talent is widening your skills gap, how can you utilize your older workers to bridge that gap? The real challenge lies in figuring out how to adapt HR policies to retain older workers. One possibility is to offer something many mature workers value (such as more flexible schedules) in exchange for their learning new skills to help bridge a skills gap in your organization. (For example, one major drugstore chain keeps older workers on board and engaged [rather than headed out the door into retirement] by offering them flexibly structured positions with fewer hours—an enticement that's been very effective at helping managers and HR executives staff difficult-to-fill retail positions.) What other incentives can you offer to existing older workers? Also consider whether there are demographic changes occurring in the geographic area where your company is located that can affect your employee base.

The ability to understand and respond to consumer demands is critical to your company's future survival, and as many HR executives are figuring out, it will take outside-of-the-box thinking to ensure that your workforce is prepared to meet your customers' needs. Linking your company's projected growth to the makeup of your workforce can safeguard your organization's relevance now and in the future. Figuring out answers to these questions can arm you with the data you need to approach your top executives. If you can clearly demonstrate that such policies will have a positive effect on the company's bottom line, you're more likely to get senior management on board with enacting policies that support the endeavors and goals of an age-diverse workforce.

THE CHANGING ROLE OF THE EMPLOYEE

These days, the ideal employee isn't someone who's good—or even great—at his or her job. The ideal employee is someone who not only excels at his or her work but also understands how to be part of a diverse workforce.

At the time I first started working as an engineer at Allison Gas Turbine, the company had two employees who were among the very few subject-matter experts in a highly technical field. Their specialized knowledge and skill sets allowed them to get away with inappropriate behavior (such as yelling at other employees or giving attitude to their bosses), because management considered them "too smart to let go." By the time I left Allison several years later, though, the company had replaced those two employees with individuals who were not only good at their jobs but who had been hired specifically because they were also able to get along with their fellow employees. What many companies (including Allison) have learned in the past decade or two is that great companies are built on many great individuals working together. Arrogant hotshots are less tolerated now, even if they have valuable skills, because their bad behavior can adversely affect the entire company in numerous ways, such as driving away great employees or making the organization vulnerable to lawsuits. Having a subject-matter expert or rainmaker on board can be fantastic for the company—as long as he or she understands the importance of getting along with others in the workplace.

Does that mean you need to stifle differing opinions or refrain from saying what you mean? Hardly. In fact, one reason to diversify your employee base (not just in age but in many other ways, such as ethnicity and gender, among others) is so that different experiences can weigh in on business decisions—these multiple perspectives can ensure that you're bringing the best ideas to the table. Homogenous groups have homogenous viewpoints. Although diversification can expand the knowledge and experience base that can yield ideas for future growth and broadening the customer base, keep in mind that inviting differing opinions means you must be open to new ideas and embrace the differences that arise.

BUILDING ON THESE CHANGES

Based on its 2015 survey of over 7,000 business and HR leaders in over 130 countries throughout the world, Deloitte has identified the greatest challenges for businesses today:

- Culture and engagement
- Leadership
- Learning and development[11]

At the heart of every company lies its culture, which sets the tone for how the employees are treated (by both management and each other), which in turn sets the tone for how those employees treat customers. If employees feel disposable or poorly treated (particularly by senior leaders), they will reproduce those negative feelings in their interactions among themselves as well as those with clients. The converse also holds true: employees who feel valued will then spread that sentiment to others. Culture matters because it has such a strong effect on every transaction (both internal and external) relevant to a company, and managers who underestimate its importance do so at their peril.

The link between culture and the issues of a multigenerational workplace is clear: when the company culture doesn't value the contributions of employees of all ages, the entire organization suffers. Smart company executives know that culture starts at the top and will focus on engaging employees of all generations to put their best and brightest ideas to work for the company. Management experts often debate whether culture creates engagement or engagement leads to culture. The "which comes first" discussion is irrelevant, though, as long as senior leaders understand the power of culture to create an age-*unbiased* environment.

But merely proclaiming "Now we're inclusive!" won't take a company very far. Without human capital processes in place to truly support a change in management philosophy, an organization can't accurately claim to be a welcoming and inclusive multigenerational workplace. Developing those processes requires an understanding of each generation's background, interests, and motivations (while still recognizing, of course, that such understandings take a back seat to awareness of individuals' needs). Let's take a close look at the characteristics and goals of each generation.

NOTES

1. Steinem, Gloria. *Moving Beyond Words: Age, Rage, Sex, Power, Money, Muscles: Breaking the Boundaries of Gender.* New York: Simon & Schuster, 1994, 274.

2. Munnell, Alicia. "What Is the Average Retirement Age?" Center for Retirement Research at Boston College website. August 2011. http://crr.bc.edu/wp-content/uploads/2011/08/IB_11-11-508.pdf.

3. Fry, Richard. "Millennials Surpass Gen Xers as the Largest Generation in US Labor Force." Pew Research Center website. May 11, 2015. http://www.pewresearch.org/fact-tank/2015/05/11/millennials-surpass-gen-xers-as-the-largest-generation-in-u-s-labor-force/.

4. Toossi, Mitra. "Labor Force Projections to 2024: The Labor Force Is Growing, but Slowly." *Monthly Labor Review* online. December 2015. http://www.bls.gov/opub/mlr/2015/article/labor-force-projections-to-2024.htm.

5. Ibid.

6. US Census Bureau. "US Census Bureau Projections Show a Slower Growing, Older, More Diverse Nation a Half Century from Now." US Census Bureau website. December 12, 2012. http://www.census.gov/newsroom/releases/archives/population/cb12-243.html.

7. IBM. "IBM Global CEO Study: The Enterprise of the Future." IBM website. 2008. http://www-03.ibm.com/industries/ca/en/healthcare/files/2008_ibm_global_ceo_study.pdf.

8. Beck, Randall, and Jim Harter. "Why Good Managers Are So Rare." *Harvard Business Review* online. March 13, 2014. http://hbr.org/2014/03/why-good-managers-are-so-rare/.

9. CareerBuilder. "More Than One-Quarter of Managers Said They Weren't Ready to Lead When They Began Managing Others, Finds New Career-Builder Survey." CareerBuilder website. March 28, 2011. http://www.careerbuilder.com/share/aboutus/pressreleasesdetail.aspx?id=pr626&sd=3%2F28%2F2011&ed=12%2F31%2F2011.

10. Finn, Dennis, and Anne Donavan. "PwC's NextGen: A Global Generational Study." PwC website. 2013. http://www.pwc.com/gx/en/hr-management-services/publications/assets/pwc-nextgen.pdf.

11. Bersin, Josh, Jason Geller, Nicky Wakefield, and Brett Walsh. "Introduction—The New Organization." In *Global Human Capital Trends 2016.* Westlake, TX: Deloitte University Press, 2015. http://www2.deloitte.com/us/en/pages/human-capital/articles/introduction-human-capital-trends.html.

Chapter 2

DEFINING THE GENERATIONS

We didn't have a generation gap. We had a generation Grand Canyon.
— Mary Crow Dog, *Lakota Woman*[1]

No doubt you've come across many of the descriptions used for the various generations. Baby Boomers, Echo Boomers, Generation X, Generation Y, Silent Generation, Me Generation—these terms appear all over the place in the media, and everyone has some sense of what they mean. But most of us would have a hard time defining them precisely, and the lack of standardized definitions can make it difficult to have productive conversations that help bridge divides among different age groups. So let's start by defining our terms.

WHAT THE EXPERTS SAY

When describing generations, most people tend to focus on dates—that is, birth years. The usual practice is to lump into one generation everyone who was born between year X and year Y. Sure, that's a convenient way to draw the lines. The Harvard Joint Center for Housing Studies, for example, specifically chooses "equal 20-year age spans" when defining post–World War II generations because those groups align both "with typically published age groups" and "with levels of annual births."[2] But going by the calendar alone doesn't yield an accurate picture, because a generation is defined by much more than its birth dates.

Broadly speaking, a generation can be characterized as "an identifiable group that shares birth years, age, location, and significant life events at critical developmental stages."[3] The Pew Research Center, a social-science research organization that specializes in demographic research, points out that "a generation typically refers to groups of people born over a 15–20 year span" but adds that definitions of generations are ideally based on "a range of factors, including demographics, attitudes, historical events, popular culture, and prevailing consensus among researchers."[4] The Pew researchers go on to highlight three critical factors to consider when differentiating among multiple age groups:[5]

1. Life cycle effect (or age effect): "When a life cycle effect is at play, differences between younger and older people are largely due to their respective positions in the life cycle." This one is pretty easy to understand. Just think back to when you were a teenager (when you still lived at home and weren't responsible for many—or any!—bills) and compare that with what your life is like now (when you have a mortgage, a career, or a family—or all three!). No doubt you've experienced some shifts in your attitudes based on your

stage of life. Childhood, adulthood, parenthood, retirement—each of those phases has distinct concerns and outlooks.

2. Period effect: This manifests "when events and circumstances ... as well as broader social forces ... simultaneously impact everyone, regardless of age." The Great Recession of 2007–2009 is one example of such an event that touched all segments of the population. Similarly, desegregation and the civil rights movement of the 1960s also yielded society-wide effects.

3. Cohort effect: This results from "unique historical circumstances that members of an age cohort experience, particularly during a time when they are in the process of forming opinions." The Pew researchers highlight two types of cohort effects: those that "may be the result of a period effect an older generation experienced that subsequent generations did not" (for example, people who were alive on 9/11 experienced a cohort effect that people born after 9/11 did not) and those that "have an outsize effect on members of one generation" (for example, people who were in adolescence or young adulthood—two formative periods in life—during the Vietnam War experienced it differently from people who were much older or much younger than them at that time).

As you can see, when defining a generation, so much more data than birth dates must be considered! In addition to the birth dates and the three effects described earlier, other factors (such as ethnicity, religion, and marital status, to name just a few) can play a role, too. But this chapter isn't intended to provide a comprehensive analysis of generational factors and definitions (I'll leave that to the demographic researchers and other experts!). My goal here is to provide an overview of the frameworks used to define generations—and a sense of how tricky it can be to come up with rigid definitions—so the rest of this book launches from a starting point that's accessible to all readers.

So with all of that in mind, let's talk about the different generations found in today's workplace!

THE BIG THREE—AND A NEWCOMER

First off, I'm going to set some parameters. It's true that there are some pre–Baby Boomers (e.g., the Greatest Generation, the Silent Generation) collecting paychecks these days. But those folks are so few in number that most discussions about the generations in today's workplace usually omit them. I'm going to follow that trend myself and focus on the generations that make up the bulk of today's workers: Baby Boomers, Generation Xers, Millennials, and Generation Zers.[6]

As far as birth dates go, only the Baby Boomers have numbers that are pretty much universally accepted: 1946–1964. In fact, theirs is the only generation that's *officially* defined by the US Census Bureau, as one journalist found out when he called that office.[7] If you ask anyone about dates for other generations, you'll get plenty of different responses. They're usually not far off from each other, though, and tend to vary by only a few years—further proof of my earlier "everyone has some sense of what they mean" statement.

In my own research on how generations are defined, I've found that the Pew Research Center's birth date ranges tend to fall pretty much in the middle of the many variations out there. Plus, as I mentioned earlier, the Pew folks have a proven track record as experts on demographics. I have a lot of confidence in what they say on this subject, so I'm going to follow their lead and use their dates here.

Baby Boomers (1946–1964)

Unlike other generations, the generation of the Baby Boomers has tidy start and end dates. The start of the post–World War II baby boom and the introduction of the birth control pill (which prompted a sudden decline in birth rates) serve as convenient bookends for this group, which currently numbers about 76 million people.[8]

The Baby Boomers came of age during a period marked by significant civil unrest and heightened concern about international affairs, particularly the growth of communism throughout the world. The Soviet Union tested its first atomic bomb in 1949, setting the stage for the Cold War, the panic that Senator Joseph McCarthy unleashed during the 1950s over supposed communist sympathizers, the overnight construction of the Berlin Wall in 1961, and the US–Soviet conflict over Cuba that culminated in the Cuban Missile Crisis of 1962. (The Cold War wasn't *completely* bad, though—after all, it drove space exploration, which in addition to the great achievement of landing people on the moon also resulted in the development of the satellite communications technologies that we all depend on today!)

Halfway around the world, Mao Zedong's Communist Party seized control of China in 1949. A few years later, violence in Vietnam escalated as the north (backed by the Soviet Union and China) sought to reunify the country under communist rule. What began as a primarily regional conflict eventually involved the United States and early Baby Boomers, who were drafted to fight in the war there. That war cost thousands of young Americans their lives, permanently injured thousands more, and divided the nation. Many experts point to the Vietnam War as one of the most formative influences on this generation.

This generation had to contend with more than just conflict abroad, though. The Baby Boomers grew up amid dramatic social change—often fueled by conflict—domestically, too. The sexual revolution (whose start coincided with the official end of the Baby Boomers' birth years) and the civil rights movement compelled people to reconsider how they related to each other, and amid these rapidly changing political and social realities, many Baby Boomers rebelled against their more conventional parents.

War, uncertainty, and economic mobility were some of the main forces that shaped this generation. The formative years of the Baby Boomers were also marked by the assassinations of several political and social leaders: President John F. Kennedy (1963), civil rights activist and leader Martin Luther King Jr. (1968), and Senator Bobby Kennedy (1968).

Turmoil and *promise* are two hallmarks of this generation's life experiences. As young adults they were shaped by war and social upheaval and in their later years experienced the highest divorce rates and second marriages in recorded history. At the same time, though, most of the generation continued to pursue the so-called American Dream—and this pursuit (and their success at it) gave them a reputation for materialism and greediness that led to this group also being known as the Me Generation.

Generation Xers (1965–1980)

The Generation Xers weren't a huge group to begin with (thanks to their parents' low fertility rates, this generation is also known as the Baby Busters) and today number about 66 million. Although the Vietnam War was still raging when the first members of Generation X were born, its direct impact on them isn't significant enough to warrant inclusion on most lists of the major influences on this group. That's not to say that this generation didn't experience its own conflicts and difficulties during its members' formative years. Generation Xers grew up in an economic climate shaken by numerous energy crises (one in 1973, caused by the OPEC oil embargo; one in 1979, arising from the Iranian Revolution; and one in 1990, connected to the Gulf War.) And of course many of them were old enough to serve in the largest military conflict of their generation, the Gulf War.

More than any previous generation, Generation Xers grew up in dual-income and single-income households. Also known as the Latchkey Generation, they had to fend for themselves and learn to be self-sufficient early on, since they were often at home on their own. As they entered adulthood, they (and their parents) were the first to experience major corporate downsizing. Widespread political scandal (Watergate, the Iran-Contra Affair, the impeachment of President Bill Clinton) and the arrival of AIDS made them more cynical and pessimistic than their predecessors. Environmental disasters, too, such as the meltdown at Three Mile Island (1979), the Union Carbide disaster in Bhopal, India (1984), and the Chernobyl accident (1986), helped shaped their views of the world.

In spite of growing up amid the fall of the Berlin Wall, the end of the Cold War, and rapid technological growth, Generation Xers have a strong sense of skepticism about politicians and corporate leaders. As they've entered adulthood, they've witnessed the slipping of the United States's military and economic supremacy in the world, and for the first time in US history they will be financially less well-off than their predecessors.[9] Outnumbered by both the generation before and the generation after it, Generation X is often regarded as the overlooked and neglected middle child of American society.[10] This generation's life experiences are characterized by *independence* and *disillusionment*.

Millennials (1981–1997)

According to the US Census Bureau, the number of Americans born between 1982 and 2000 is just over 83 million, making it the largest segment of the population.[11] In 2015, this group became the largest segment of the US workforce, too—and that's even without including the many Millennials who are still in school and not yet counted as employees.[12] For a while this group was also known as Generation Y (because that letter follows X in the alphabet), but that name didn't stick. Some researchers prefer to call this group the Echo Boomers, because its high population puts it on par with the Baby Boomers who came two generations before them. Most experts, though, have settled on calling them Millennials.

Although many Millennials grew up in households with divorce, their Generation X parents focused intently on their children (in part to counter the absenteeism of their own parents, the Baby Boomers). More than preceding generations, Millennials lived sheltered childhoods as their attentive parents shuttled them from one scheduled activity to the next and kept them busy—and safe from negatives. In their most intense manifestations, such as helicopter parenting, their parents' efforts to protect them actually left some Millennials ill equipped for lives as fully independent adults.

That's not to say that some of that protection wasn't completely unwarranted. Millennials grew up in a climate of conflict and fear. Many of them were around during the Gulf War (1990–1991) and came of age during the Oklahoma City bombing and the September 11 attacks. The Columbine shootings were the first of what proved to be numerous mass shootings at schools, and many Millennials have had to practice lockdown drills in their classrooms. Amid all these concerns, more than any other generation the Millennials have more laws designed to protect them.

Told from birth that they are special and valued, Millennials grew up nurtured by all of the adults around them. This generation ushered in the era of "everybody gets a medal" awards for participation and was taught to expect instant rewards for its hard work. At the same time, Millennials have been encouraged to talk openly and publicly about their feelings, require lots of feedback, and eagerly want to make positive change in the world. One extensive survey of workplace Millennials offered this summary: they "call for meaning, mentorship, and meritocracy in a workplace that channels what they bring to the table."[13]

Thanks to increased educational opportunities, this is the first generation in which women outnumber men in college (and achieve higher test scores and grades than them, too!). It also happens to be a very ethnically diverse generation (43 percent of Millennials are nonwhite).[14]

With the Internet and personal computers taking over society's center stage during their childhoods, Millennials grew up with technology, earning them the nickname "digital natives." Their easy and immediate access to information and communication makes them the first truly global generation. Millennials' life experiences are characterized by *shelter* and *connection*.

Generation Zers (1998–present)

This generation is still so new that experts are only beginning to include it in demographic analyses. A few names have been thrown about for this group—Nextsters, Homeland Generation, iGeneration, and Post-Millennials are just a few—but by far the one with the most currency today among both demographic researchers and the media (and the name that I think will stick in the long run) is Generation Z. As of 2015 this group numbers about 80 million (because figures for each generation aren't precise, some surveys show it running neck and neck with or even surpassing the Millennials), but it's still growing and will soon be the largest generational group in the United States.[15] It's also the most diverse generation to date in terms of ethnicity, religion, and family structure, surpassing even the Millennials in that regard.

So far, technology is the hallmark of this group, which is "the first generation to be raised in the era of smartphones" and social media.[16] A consultant at a firm specializing in the management of Millennials compares Generation Zers to the generation that preceded them:

> Generation Z are like millennials on steroids.... They are millennials amplified. The minute they were born, they already had a domain name and a Facebook profile and Twitter feed. Social media is second nature to them. Even members of Gen Z who don't necessarily think they're tech savvy absolutely are. Technology is an extension of their self-expression.[17]

Generation Zers' high proficiency with social media benefits more than just their personal friendships, though. It's also making them "accustomed to engaging with friends all over the world, so they are well prepared for a global business environment."[18]

They're growing up amid the promise of technological innovation—but also in an environment of economic uncertainty, clouded by the recession of their childhood and a sharp decrease in the well-defined and reliable career paths and opportunities that previous generations enjoyed. Where Generation Xers and Millennials have had to modify their expectations in the wake of recessions and other option-limiting events, "Generation Z ... has had its eyes open from the beginning."[19] Consequently, when compared to their predecessors, this group is both more cautious and more anxious (particularly about paying for college and finding good jobs). So far, Generation Z's life experiences can be characterized by *technology* and *caution*.

GENERATIONAL CHARACTERISTICS

In order to manage people, you need to understand them. And because generation-based experiences and attitudes greatly influence not only how employees do their own jobs but also how they relate to other employees, anyone who manages a multigenerational workplace should prioritize understanding those experiences and attitudes.

Becoming familiar with each generation's history and major influences (as detailed already) is a good start. With that knowledge, you can get a sense of each generation's values, motivations, strengths (and shortcomings), and career goals—all information that can help you make sure that your employees are in the positions that work best for them and for your organization. For example, Baby Boomers who grew up during an era of well-defined job responsibilities and corporate loyalty might operate best with clear hierarchies and expectations, whereas socially driven Generation Zers might thrive with less-rigid structures and more entrepreneurial opportunities.

Table 2.1 outlines some of the primary characteristics and influences of the four generations discussed earlier. The information here is culled from a variety of sources, including demographic research, media analyses, and my own experience. As both an employee and a manager, you surely have your own observations as well, so feel free to add them to this table. You may also find it useful to share the information on this table with your colleagues and employees, because they, too, need to understand how to negotiate generational differences in the workplace.

THE MORE THINGS CHANGE

Back when Generation X was first entering the workforce, in the early 1980s, most every news story proclaimed them disrespectful cynics unwilling to embrace the country's traditional work ethic. "Why are today's young people so skeptical?" asked *Time*, while an article written by *Newsweek* staffers decried them as "The Whiny Generation" and a *Washington Post* headline chided them to "Grow Up, Crybabies."

Fast-forward nearly two decades and the media is playing the same tune—only this time it's a remix featuring Millennials. A March 2014 feature in *The Atlantic* cited a study describing Gen X's successors as "deeply confused" and "contradictory," while Jean Twenge, Ph.D., professor in the Department of Psychology at San Diego State University, conducted several not-so-flattering studies on Millennials that she incorporated into her book, *Generation Me: Why Today's Young Americans Are More Confident, Assertive, Entitled—and More Miserable Than Ever Before*, whose title is just as telling as that of her follow-up, *The Narcissism Epidemic: Living in the Age of Entitlement*. *Wired* even acknowledged the trend to denigrate the next generation with an article entitled "Congrats, Millennials. It's Your Turn to Be Vilified."

The more things change, the more things stay the same.

Table 2.1 Generational Influences and Attributes

	Baby Boomers	Generation Xers	Millennials	Generation Zers
Birth years	1946–1964	1965–1980	1981–1997	1998–present
Population	76 million	66 million	83 million	80 million (and growing)
Influential events and trends (period effects and cohort effects)	Cold War spread of communism Vietnam War sexual revolution civil rights movement assassinations of political/ cultural leaders	energy crises political scandals corporate downsizing AIDS environmental disasters decline of US world supremacy Internet and e-mail *Challenger* disaster	September 11 attacks school shootings busy schedules sheltered/ protected by parents social media	school shootings global terrorism (notably Al-Qaeda and ISIS) increased social diversity (e.g., ethnic- ity, religion, family structure)
General traits and charac- teristics	team oriented optimistic formal	self-reliant cynical informal	feedback oriented community oriented realistic	globally oriented extremely tech savvy pragmatic socially progressive
Work/career goals	long-term stability clear hierarchies few or zero job changes	work-life balance only necessary job changes flexible schedules	entrepreneurial opportunities clear directions frequent job changes fun workplaces	lifetime work (not reliance on social safety pro- grams to fund retirement)
Communi- cation and tech	phone, fax, e-mail, introduced to Internet and personal computers as adults	e-mail, texting introduced to Internet and personal computers as children and young adults	e-mail, texting digital natives grew up with Internet and personal computers	texting, social media "'Internet-in-its- pocket' generation" born into Inter- net world, grew up with mobile devices

Table 2.1 (continued)

	Baby Boomers	Generation Xers	Millennials	Generation Zers
Workplace strengths	team players willing to put in extra effort	not bound by structure adaptable	technologically adept eager to make an impact on the world	technologically adept independent value long-term professional development
Workplace weaknesses	difficulty dealing with conflict trouble thinking outside the box	less personal investment in jobs rejection of structure and rules	need for structure, supervision, and validation unrealistic expectations for interesting work lack of experience	short attention spans lack of experience

NOTES

1. Excerpt from *Lakota Woman*, copyright © 1990 by Mary Dog Crow and Richard Erdoes. Used by permission of Gove/Atlantic, Inc. Any third-party use of this material, outside of this publication, is prohibited.
2. Masnick, George. "Defining Generations." *Housing Perspectives: Research, Trends, and Perspectives from the Harvard Joint Center for Housing Studies* (blog). November 28, 2012. http://housingperspectives.blogspot.com/2012/11/defining_generations.html.
3. Tobize, Anick. "Generational Differences in the Workplace." Research and Training Center on Community Living at the University of Minnesota website. August 16, 2008. http://rtc.umn.edu/docs/2_18_Gen_diff_workplace.pdf.
4. Pew Research Center. "The Whys and Hows of Generations Research." Pew Research Center website. September 3, 2015. http://www.people-press.org/2015/09/03/the-whys-and-hows-of-generations-research/.
5. Ibid.
6. These are the most common names used in corporate America and online.
7. Bump, Philip. "Here Is When Each Generation Begins and Ends, According to Facts." *The Atlantic* online. March 25, 2014. http://www.theatlantic.com/national/archive/2014/03/here-is-when-each-generation-begins-and-ends-according-to-facts/359589/.

8. Colby, Sandra L., and Jennifer M. Ortman. "The Baby Boom Cohort in the United States: 2012 to 2060." US Census Bureau website. May 2014. http://www.census.gov/prod/2014pubs/p25-1141.pdf.

9. Fry, Richard. "This Year Millennials Will Overtake Baby Boomers." Pew Research Center website. January 16, 2015. http://www.pewresearch.org/fact-tank/2015/01/16/this-year-millennials-will-overtake-baby-boomers/.

10. Taylor, Paul, and George Gao. "Generation X: America's Neglected 'Middle Child.'" Pew Research Center website. June 5, 2014. http://www.pewresearch.org/fact-tank/2014/06/05/generation-x-americas-neglected-middle-child/.

11. US Census Bureau. "Millennials Outnumber Baby Boomers and Are Far More Diverse, Census Bureau Reports." US Census Bureau website. June 25, 2015. http://www.census.gov/newsroom/press-releases/2015/cb15-113.html.

12. Fry, Richard. "Millennials Surpass Gen Xers as the Largest Generation in US Labor Force." Pew Research Center website. May 11, 2015. http://www.pewresearch.org/fact-tank/2015/05/11/millennials-surpass-gen-xers-as-the-largest-generation-in-u-s-labor-force/.

13. Hillhouse, Alison. "Consumer Insights: MTV's 'No Collar Workers.'" *Blog .Viacom* (blog). October 4, 2012. http://blog.viacom.com/2012/10/consumer-insights-mtvs-no-collar-workers/.

14. Pew Research Center. "Millennials in Adulthood." Pew Research Center website. March 7, 2014. http://www.pewsocialtrends.org/2014/03/07/millennials-in-adulthood/.

15. Dill, Kathryn. "7 Things Employers Should Know About the Gen Z Workforce." *Forbes* online. November 6, 2015. http://www.forbes.com/sites/kathryndill/2015/11/06/7-things-employers-should-know-about-the-gen-z-workforce.html.

16. Williams, Alex. "Move Over, Millennials, Here Comes Generation Z." *The New York Times* online. September 18, 2015. http://www.nytimes.com/2015/09/20/fashion/move-over-millennials-here-comes-generation-z.html.

17. Knowledge@Wharton. "'Millennials on Steroids': Is Your Brand Ready for Generation Z?" Knowledge@Wharton website. September 28, 2015. http://knowledge.wharton.upenn.edu/article/millennials-on-steroids-is-your-brand-ready-for-generation-z/.

18. Levit, Alexandra. "Make Way for Generation Z." *The New York Times* online. March 28, 2015. http://www.nytimes.com/2015/03/29/jobs/make-way-for-generation-z.html\LY1\textbackslash.

19. Williams, Alex. "Move Over, Millennials, Here Comes Generation Z." *The New York Times* online. September 18, 2015. http://www.nytimes.com/2015/09/20/fashion/move-over-millennials-here-comes-generation-z.html.

Chapter 3

FOSTERING A CULTURE OF INCLUSION

Employers have recognized for some time that it's smart business to have a diverse workforce—one in which many views are represented and everyone's talents are valued.

—Thomas Perez, "Our New Year's Resolution"[1]

M any company leaders talk about embracing diversity, but such conversations typically focus on ethnicity and gender and often neglect to address age. Although discrimination on the basis of ethnicity and gender is indeed a problem in the workplace, age discrimination is also a very real problem—especially for older workers. In a 2013 AARP survey of individuals aged 45 to 74, 64 percent of respondents said they "have seen or experienced age discrimination in the workplace," with 58 percent saying they believe it starts when a person reaches his or her 50s.[2] This environment is shaped in part by the fact that many influential leaders perpetuate the stereotype that younger is better. At the 2011 NASCOMM (National Association for Software and Services Companies) Product Enclave, for example, venture capital investor Vinod Khosla told attendees, "People under 35 are the people who make change happen" and "People over 45 basically die in terms of new ideas" in part because they "[fall] back on old habits."[3] This perception isn't entirely accurate, though, and the data tell a different story—in particular, research by Benjamin Jones of the Kellogg School of Management at Northwestern University, which found that life experiences give someone 50 and older significantly more innovation potential than a 25-year-old.[4] Indeed, the over-50 crowd is one of the fastest growing groups of entrepreneurs in the United States.

What does that mean for organizations? Savvy companies can benefit from older workers' proclivity for innovation by keeping those employees alongside younger workers who can help drive that innovation. (McDonald's, for example, understands this mission: it reported a 20 percent increase in performance in locations where staff aged 60+ work alongside younger employees.)[5] But keeping aging workers around is only one way to address management challenges. It's also critical to create an environment in which employees of all ages are engaged and focused on rethinking the company's products and services in order to meet changing consumer expectations. Companies should not underestimate the value of employee engagement: a Gallup study found that "engaged employees are far more likely to suggest or develop creative ways to improve management or business processes."[6] The key is to foster an environment of inclusion that recognizes differences, celebrates commonalities, and puts into action policies and procedures that address each group's priorities. Doing so can yield benefits for businesses of all sizes.

That's easier said than done, though, particularly in large, well-established organizations, because their tendency to emphasize making existing products in a consistent and cost-efficient manner often makes them less likely to innovate.[7] Under such a drive for reliability, employees focus on maximizing efficiency—and not dreaming up new products and services. Vinod Khosla's comments would be accurate if they were restated as *"Companies* basically die in terms of new ideas" because they rely "on old habits," and employees (particularly those who have been with the organization the longest) follow the leadership's example.

THE BUSINESS CASE FOR DIVERSITY

Even as you embrace a multigenerational workforce to support innovation, it's important to understand that age diversity (or diversity of any kind) and inclusion can only become priorities in your company if senior leaders make those goals company-wide business initiatives. To be effective, diversity initiatives must carry the same weight as other business goals, such as increasing market share or decreasing cost of goods sold. Many companies recognize this already: in a Forbes Insights study on workplace diversity that surveyed 321 executives at global companies with annual revenues in excess of $500 million, the overwhelming majority of the respondents reported a positive correlation between diversity and innovation. The director of global diversity and inclusion at Intel, Rosalind Hudnell, underscores the connection: "You can't be successful on a global stage without [diversity]."[8]

In a 2014 survey by the Chartered Institute of Personnel and Development (CIPD), both employees and employers raised numerous positives about working in age-diverse teams. Employers pointed to "knowledge sharing (55 percent [of respondents]), enhanced customer service (14 percent), and greater innovation (7 percent) as the key benefits of age-diverse teams." Employees, on the other hand, highlighted other benefits, including "having different perspectives (72 percent), knowledge-sharing (66 percent), new ideas (41 percent) and improved problem solving (32 percent)."[9] A 2013 study of 24 companies with strong reputations for making diversity a priority found that having a highly diverse team enabled an organization to come up with a wider range of solutions to business problems because the team members challenged each other more. Prior to diversifying, it was observed that a nondiverse workforce becomes too insular and out of touch with its (more diverse) customer base.[10]

If diversity has such a positive impact on employee engagement and innova-tion efforts, why don't all organizations embrace such efforts? One possible reason lies in an observation by the Forbes Insights study that "[generational] differences, if not addressed, can be disruptive and lead to serious misunderstandings."[11] In other words, once a workplace becomes more diverse, managers have to work harder to make sure everyone gets along—and managing employees is already difficult enough even without a workforce that spans multiple generations. However, as data increasingly supports the case for increased diversity and inclusion, it is critical that senior leaders and managers alike value positive contributions from whomever or wherever they come. A workforce that feels thus appreciated will be more engaged—an attitude that can have a positive impact on the company's bottom line.

THE ROLE OF COMPANY CULTURE

If you've been in the workforce for even a short amount of time, you've probably encountered different company cultures—and you've likely fit in with some of them better than with others. When an employee is a good match with a particular company's culture, he or she is more likely to thrive in that environment. When the employee and the culture don't get along, though, that relationship isn't likely to last long. I learned this lesson firsthand when I moved from a small organization in which I had a lot of freedom to a large company (owned by an even bigger conglomerate). Its culture was much more rigid to the point that I practically had to ask for permission just to go to the bathroom! That sort of environment is a complete cultural mismatch for me, and it was a miracle I survived there as long as I did (six months—and I was miserable the whole time). That experience helped me understand how corporate culture can play a strong role in getting the best from employees.

Howard Schultz, the CEO of Starbucks, highlighted the value of culture in his 2011 book, *Onward: How Starbucks Fought for Its Life without Losing Its Soul*. He writes that after he stepped down from the helm of Starbucks in 2000, the company strayed from its original people-focused company culture, values, and mission. By adopting a business strategy that emphasized expansion at all costs, the company saw its revenues and stock prices fall precipitously.[12] When Schultz returned as CEO in 2008 to revive the faltering company, he led a massive turnaround effort that put the focus back on people—customers and (notably) employees—and led to record earnings just five years later. In describing the company's new success, Schultz famously declared, "Culture trumps strategy."[13]

Companies that achieve long-term success share one vital characteristic: they are full of employees and managers who feel valued and constantly push themselves to meet—and exceed—their goals. This drive arises from personal accountability, which must be present at all levels in an organization (from the CEO to the receptionist) in order for the company to succeed. Managers who want their employees to demonstrate personal accountability must lead by example. This is particularly important when it comes to fostering an inclusive environment: if *you* don't demonstrate respect for employees of all ages and value *everyone's* input, why should they?

Merriam-Webster defines accountability as "the quality or state of being accountable; *esp*: an obligation or willingness to accept responsibility or to account for one's actions."[14] *Even in the face of challenges*, employees with a high degree of personal accountability feel compelled to help the company succeed as well as internally obligated to complete projects or fulfill tasks to which they have committed. Personal accountability is a choice and an attitude that manifests in an individual's actions to own the issues and their outcomes (both good and bad).

So what's the connection between personal accountability and the creation of an inclusive work environment? When C-suite (CEO, CFO, COO, etc.) executives make diversity and inclusion more than just "nice to have" features and treat them as "must have" business requirements that align with the company's core objectives, employees who have a high degree of personal accountability will take note. For those employees, whatever the leadership deems a "must have" becomes their personal goal—and they will work hard to achieve it.

As you consider joining a particular company (or as you look to increase your leadership acumen in your current organization), it's important to understand how a company's culture plays a critical role in supporting (or undermining) an individual manager's ability to lead. Company culture isn't just a clever motto plastered on the wall or an inspirational quote handed to employees on a laminated card. It comprises the values, beliefs, and (perhaps most importantly) the behaviors that are exhibited and shared by the majority of the organization's employees. Company culture isn't what the organization *proclaims* about itself, but what it actually *practices* in its day-to-day functioning. It includes the beliefs employees share regarding their worth to the company, how things *really* get accomplished, and what the company values when awarding promotions and other opportunities.

As previously mentioned, corporate culture originates at the senior-most levels of an organization. Just as ripples spread across a pond after a rock is thrown in the water, the C-suite's methods of valuing and rewarding its direct reports influence the remaining employees' responses. If your CEO exhibits finger-pointing tendencies, for example, chances are his or her direct reports will follow suit and display the same behavior with *their* direct reports—and so on down the chain of command. Similarly, when senior leaders favor (or disfavor) one age group, leaders farther down the command chain may have a hard time opposing that attitude. When senior leaders demonstrate respect for the input of all age groups, this support permeates the organization and is modeled by people at all levels (and thus becomes a part of the company culture). Employees who know that their contributions are valued are likely to be more engaged in the workplace—and high employee engagement can yield great dividends for the company's bottom line.

So where should you start if you want to improve your company culture? CEOs and other senior leaders who want to capitalize on the benefits of having a culture of inclusivity first need to assess the current state of their organizations. After all, they can't decide where they want the company to be in the future if they don't know where it is now. Remember, before launching any initiatives to promote diversity around age (or other demographic factor), it's important to first link them to the company's strategic goals so that the initiatives are truly "must have" and not just "nice to have." To help you make that connection when planning such a program (and thus demonstrate that it's a business imperative), consider the following questions:

- What is the current composition of your customer base? What will your customer base look like in five years? What potential customers should you target to continue a growth trajectory?
- What is the current composition of your employee base, and how might that be different in five years? Does your employee base reflect similar professional organizations in your field?

Understanding who your current and future customers are and aligning those groups with your current and future employee bases can give you insight into potential opportunities for diversified hiring to target untapped markets. Research upholds the value of having an age-diverse workforce: in one survey of 100,000 workers, "42 percent of respondents said that the differences between Gen Y (Millennials), Gen Xers, and Boomers actually improved productivity in the workplace."[15] Because there's a strong correlation between productivity and business opportunities, deficiencies in your employee base that lead to reduced productivity at your organization can in turn lead to opportunities for other companies to tap into your potential market share. When assessing the state of your workforce, consider these questions:

- What leadership capabilities will be needed to motivate and engage your workforce in five years? Is your current employee base developing the skill sets to achieve those future leadership requirements?
- What other skill sets are missing in your employees' tool kits, and what is the plan to develop those skills? How is succession planning being addressed as the company grows?
- Do you have a critical employee population retiring in 5 to 10 years? What is being done to bridge any skills gaps that result when they leave the company?
- Do you have a formal recognition program that rewards getting along with coworkers of all ages? If so, is that program age-blind, or does it tend to recognize one age group of workers the most? How can you ensure that all ages are equally valued?
- As the skills gap increases, how can older workers' skill sets be retooled and Millennial and Generation X employees be prepared to fill those gaps? How will your company sustain momentum in innovation over the long term?
- What changes to the work environment will be needed to achieve your company's business objectives now and in the future?

In boardrooms across the United States, there's more and more talk about how American companies are losing their entrepreneurial edge because of consolidation and competition from foreign competitors.[16] Such talk is of great concern to senior leaders, who know that an organization's continued success depends on innovation and risk-taking to keep the company relevant in the future. Indeed, a joint study by IESE Business School of the University of Navarra and Capgemini Consulting found that companies with greater amounts of innovation enjoyed greater financial performance.[17] Engagement, too, can have an impact on the bottom line: a 2015 study by AARP found that "it takes only a 5 percent increase in engagement to achieve 3 percent incremental revenue growth."[18] Figuring out how to take advantage of the skill sets of current employees (especially more mature workers who are inclined to innovate) will help your company gain a competitive edge now and in the future.

- Are your current employees capable of making innovations to lead your company in the near (and far) future? What hiring and training decisions need to be made now in order to meet your future innovation needs?
- Are hiring decisions made by a multigenerational team? Do promotional opportunities favor a particular age group?

Hiring employees from varying age groups is one step toward increasing workplace diversity (and, therefore, increasing a company's capability for innovation). After all, when the success of a department or organization is at stake, does it really matter where great ideas come from? A stellar idea can come from someone who just joined the workforce or from someone who's been with the company for decades. For that reason, managing in the new workplace reality means prioritizing the creation of a culture of inclusion that supports innovation from employees of any age.

OVERCOMING A NEGATIVE CULTURE

What if your senior leaders set a bad example and create a negative corporate culture? Although it is possible to mitigate the influence of a CEO who displays negative behavior, it can be difficult to do so throughout an entire company. Individual departments can be pockets of positivity and inclusivity, but a few positive environments aren't enough to reshape the entire company's culture. For a company to reap the financial benefits of a positive corporate culture, *all* of its employees (regardless of age or other demographic characteristic) must be treated with respect. All employees must feel valued—a state that can be difficult to accomplish if the leadership is throwing stones that send negative ripples throughout the company.

It's important to note that if the senior leadership at your organization is setting a bad example, that does not give managers a license to behave in the same manner—at least, not if they want to keep their best performers. "People join companies but leave managers" (as the old saying goes), so managers must never underestimate how much their actions influence employee retention. Because new hires typically take four to six months to get up to speed, managers whose management style leads to constant employee churn will never reap the rewards of having fully trained employees. As a manager, your goal (regardless of your senior leaders' actions) is to create an environment in which your employees are engaged, motivated, and performing at their best—and creating such an environment includes valuing employees of all ages.

It's definitely in your best interest to be the best manager you can be. In addition to the overall goal of helping the company succeed, keep in mind that when your employees perform well, they make *you* look good! (And of course, when they perform poorly, they make you look bad.) Stepping up your management game will also help you attract the brightest and best employees to work for you: good news travels fast! So if your senior executives are poor leaders, do everything you can to make sure their bad behavior stops with you and doesn't progress farther down the chain of command.

CREATING AN AGE-DIVERSE CULTURE

The secret to creating an age-diverse culture (or a culture that's diverse in other ways) is to hire candidates of diverse backgrounds. Sounds simple, right? The real challenge is finding diverse candidates. To do that, you need to expand your candidate pool for various positions. Unfortunately, the usual hiring practices don't favor hiring for diversity; because people are predisposed to hire people like themselves, what usually happens is like hires like. Therefore, to create a diverse culture a company's HR and hiring managers must look beyond the usual talent pools to find potential candidates.

With the Internet providing access to nearly the entire world, it's easier than ever for today's managers and HR staff to increase the diversity of their candidate pools by pushing beyond "old school" channels and exploring the ever-expanding list of newer options for reaching out to candidates. The next step is to create an age-blind hiring process that focuses on the *proficiencies* needed to succeed in a particular position and assesses candidates based on how well they meet those requirements. Yes, likability and personality do matter when making hiring decisions. But if an employee ends up being terminated because of an inability to do the job, then his or her likability is irrelevant. Of course, companies are legally prohibited from discriminating based on certain characteristics (including age) when hiring. An organization's goal should not be just to comply with those laws but rather to hire with blinders on to shut out everything except a candidate's ability to do the job itself.

Just as companies look for candidates who are diverse in age and other characteristics, though, candidates look for organizations that have diverse workforces. Today, an inclusive environment is no longer an anomaly in the business world—it's an expectation. For example, almost half of the respondents in one extensive survey said they "want their employers to deploy real solutions to foster and enforce a diverse work environment."[19] Having an inclusive environment will thus help you not only retain your current employees but also (because referrals play such a huge role in hiring) attract candidates who are more likely to succeed in your organization. Once you've hired well and have an age-diverse workforce in place, you can implement strategies to motivate and engage those employees for improved innovation. First, you need to encourage them to pursue the following:

- **Risk-taking:** the act or fact of doing something that involves danger or risk in order to achieve a goal[20]
- **Innovation:** a new idea, device, or method[21]
- **Entrepreneurship:** the capacity and willingness to develop, organize, and manage a business venture along with any of its risks in order to make a profit[22]

Critical to an organization's success, these three activities embody an approach that compels an employee (regardless of his or her age) to engage in creative problem solving and to actively pursue a better way of operating rather than merely follow along with business as usual. Employees who exhibit an entrepreneurial spirit don't just wait for change to come to them—they seek out positive change that improves the company's culture or function.

But innovation doesn't just happen: it needs to be nurtured, supported, and protected (particularly, as often happens, when ideas don't come to fruition). To achieve this innovative attitude and allow it to thrive in an organization, a company must support it—and that support must start at the top. Even the senior-most executive (let alone a middle manager) would have a hard time promoting innovation, risk-taking, and an entrepreneurial spirit if his or her efforts weren't supported by the rest of the C-suite team. So when promoting these behaviors in your own company, ask your executive team members to lead the way with their own direct reports. The following eight strategies can help spread a drive for innovation throughout your organization.

Stimulate Idea Generation

When I was the vice president of operations at Oxygen Media, my team and I held quarterly brainstorming sessions that were unrelated to our day-to-day business. In these meetings, we focused on identifying critical tasks and new approaches that weren't already on our to-do lists. This no-holds-barred, no-idea-is-a-bad-idea kind of meeting resulted in our operations team constantly being on the cutting edge of change and reinvention. It was also *incredibly* exciting for the team members to see great ideas coming from employees of all ages, and served as a powerful reminder to the entire staff that age (young, old, or somewhere in between) is not a barrier to breakthroughs.

Protect Idea Generators

If you've ever been in a meeting and proposed a new idea that was instantly attacked, you probably learned pretty quickly to keep your mouth shut so you don't get shot down. Whether you are leading the team or are merely a team member, support the crazy-idea generators who push everyone beyond their normal mode of thinking. Even just saying "Great idea! Who's next?" (instead of "We've already tried that" or "That won't work") encourages brainstorming—and can lead to some amazing answers! During brainstorming sessions, keep the tone positive by prohibiting everyone from using the words *no, but,* or *can't*. This restriction is particularly important to have in place when the team includes newer members who might suggest an idea that the department has heard (and maybe even tried unsuccessfully) before. Even an old idea is new to someone at some point, and that person might be the one to come up with a way to make it work!

Don't Slaughter Someone for Mistakes

When one of his business associates commented on how thousands of efforts to produce a new type of battery hadn't yielded results, Thomas Edison replied, "Results? Why, I have gotten a lot of results! I know several thousand [ways] that won't work!"[23] The world is made richer by failure (Post-it notes and penicillin are two classic examples of this phenomenon), and both innovation and entrepreneurial spirit die when mistakes are punished or ignored. Whether you've inherited a group of employees or have just joined a new organization in a management capacity, you may need to encourage current employees (especially those who have been around for a while) to step out of their comfort zones and assure them that you won't automatically dole out punishment for failures. The fact that it's okay to make mistakes can be a new concept to both older workers (who are long accustomed to being evaluated for their work) and younger workers (who were recently still in school environments in which getting everything right—and making no mistakes—was the primary measure of success).

Promote Good Ideas

In addition to supporting idea generators, you also need to promote good ideas, regardless of who presents them. This can be challenging in corporate America, where both leaders and employees can be sensitive about their turf. If you think like an owner (another entrepreneurial mindset), you don't care *where* great ideas originate—but you're smart enough to recognize and implement them. If you're new to managing employees, it's particularly critical not to take credit for their ideas. Not only is that unethical, but it's also counterproductive: if you promote and reward those contributions instead, you'll encourage more of the same behavior.

Broaden Your Knowledge Base

The old adage "Knowledge is power" definitely applies to fostering an entrepreneurial spirit. Whether they occupy senior roles or are influencers in junior positions, leaders must constantly expand their knowledge bases in order to know more about their organizations. The more you understand how what you do affects other operations in the company, the more able you'll be to make informed decisions that help the entire organization. It's also critical for you and your team to understand how your company makes money so you can help improve its bottom line. In every management position I held, for example, I instituted quarterly lunches to which everyone in my department was invited to hear other department heads discuss their operations, including their impact on the company's bottom line. At each of those companies, it was amazing to see how these meetings inspired my staff to think beyond their own day-to-day responsibilities.

Push Yourself beyond Your Comfort Zone

We all know that it can be hard to speak up when you're in a junior role. Interestingly, though, it can be just as challenging to speak up when you're in a senior position—after all, no one wants to make a fool of himself or herself. That's why it's important to keep learning so you can continue to make contributions throughout the company, not just in your own spheres of influence. So push yourself to break out of your day-to-day routines and responsibilities. Think beyond yourself, beyond your department, and especially beyond your comfort zone to lead change and innovation at your company.

Employ Diverse Employees and Teams

Workplace diversity is an often-discussed subject for good reason: if you want the widest array of ideas, you need people with different viewpoints and different ways of thinking. If everyone has had the same life experiences or is the same age, your team may get mired in homogeneous groupthink. So to promote innovative, creative thinking in line with an entrepreneurial spirit, make sure that your team members reflect diversity in gender, ethnicity, age, experience, and other factors that can influence how they see the world.

Recognize and Reward Risk-Taking

Even if you're not the boss in your department, chiming in with encouragement— particularly in front of others—helps to promote and support an innovative spirit. Something simple can have a *big* impact. So say "Awesome idea!" or "Thank you" in a meeting, or send that e-mail telling another employee that his or her risk inspired you. Regardless of your position in the company, acknowledging and appreciating risk-taking can have positive, far-reaching effects throughout your organization.

The psychologist Abraham Maslow stated that "an individual would engage in learning only to the extent he is not crippled by fear and to the extent he feels safe enough to dare."[24] If you want your employees to innovate, they need to feel "safe enough to dare"—willing to embrace risk and uncertainty. Promoting innovation can have a profound impact on your company. In fact, innovation may be just what your organization needs to stay ahead of its competitors (rather than try to keep up with them).

So engage your senior leaders now in figuring out how to support and encourage innovation at all levels throughout the organization! Innovation can thrive in a workplace that fosters a culture of inclusion and welcomes ideas and suggestions from everyone, no matter how old he or she is. Such a culture values the experiences and perspectives of employees of all ages and keeps them focused on the company's future.

NOTES

1. Perez, Thomas. "Our New Year's Resolution," US Department of Labor blog, December 30, 2013. http://blog.dol.gov/2013/12/30/our-new-years-resolution/.

2. AARP. "Staying Ahead of the Curve 2013: AARP Multicultural Work and Career Study: Perceptions of Age Discrimination in the Workplaces—Ages 45–74." AARP website. April 2014. http://www.aarp.org/content/dam/aarp/research/surveys_statistics/econ/2013/Staying-Ahead-of-the-Curve-Age-Discrimination.pdf.

3. Wadhwa, Vivek. "The Case for Old Entrepreneurs." *The Washington Post* online. December 2, 2011. http://www.washingtonpost.com/national/on-innovations/the-case-for-old-entrepreneurs/2011/12/02/gIQAulJ3KO_story.html.

4. Jones, Benjamin F. "Age and Great Invention." *Review of Economics and Statistics* 92, no. 1 (2010): 1–14.

5. Lancaster University. "Research Shows McDonalds Customers Prefer Older Workers." August 21, 2009. Lancaster University website. http://news.lancs.ac.uk/Web/News/Pages/BE8CC3DC5B5D9A3880257619003619DE.aspx.

6. Krueger, Jerry, and Emily Killham. "Who's Driving Innovation at Your Company?" *Gallup* website. September 14, 2006. http://www.gallup.com/businessjournal/24472/whos-driving-innovation-your-company.aspx.

7. Ashkenas, Ron. "Steve Blank on Why Companies Can't Innovate." *Harvard Business Review* online. February 13, 2013. http://hbr.org/2013/02/steve-blank-on-why-big-companies.html.

8. *Forbes* Insights. "Global Diversity and Inclusion: Fostering Innovation through a Diverse Workforce." *Forbes* website. 2011. http://images.forbes.com/forbesinsights/StudyPDFs/Innovation_Through_Diversity.pdf.

9. Chartered Institute of Personnel and Development. "Managing an Age-Diverse Workforce: Employer and Employee Views." Chartered Institute of

Personnel and Development website. 2014. http://www.cipd.co.uk/binaries/managing-an-age-diverse-workforce_2014.pdf.

10. Groysberg, Boris, and Katherine Connolly. "Great Leaders Who Make the Mix Work." *Harvard Business Review* online. September 2013. http://www.hbr.org/2013/09/great-leaders-who-make-the-mix-work/ar/1.

11. *Forbes* Insights. "Global Diversity and Inclusion: Fostering Innovation through a Diverse Workforce." *Forbes* website. 2011. http://images.forbes.com/forbesinsights/StudyPDFs/Innovation_Through_Diversity.pdf.

12. Schultz, Howard. *Onward: How Starbucks Fought for Its Life without Losing Its Soul.* New York: Rodale, 2011.

13. Helm, Leslie. "Howard Schultz." *Delta Sky* online. March 2014. http://www.deltaskymag.delta.com/Sky-Extras/Favorites/Howard-Schultz.aspx.

14. *Merriam-Webster's Collegiate Dictionary,* 11th ed.

15. Hannam, Susan, and Bonni Yordi. "Engaging a Multi-Generational Workforce: Practical Advice for Government Managers." IBM Center for the Business of Government website. Spring/Summer 2011. http://www.businessofgovernment.org/sites/default/files/Hannam_Yordi.pdf.

16. Garland, Eric. "Why America Is Losing Its Entrepreneurial Edge." *Harvard Business Review* online. May 20, 2014. http://www.hbr.org/2014/05/why-america-is-losing-its-entrepreneurial-edge/.

17. Miller, Paddy, et al. "Innovation Leadership Study: Managing Innovation: An Insider Perspective." Capgemini website, 2012. http://www.capgemini.com/resource-file-access/resource/pdf/Innovation_Leadership_Study_____Managing_innovation__An_insider_perspective.pdf.

18. AARP. "A Business Case for Workers 50+: A Look at the Value of Experience." AARP website. August 2015. http://states.aarp.org/wp-content/uploads/2015/08/A-Business-Case-for-Older-Workers-Age-50-A-Look-at-the-Value-of-Experience.pdf.

19. Goldstein, Melanie. "The Impact of Workplace Diversity from the Employee Perspective." Kanjoya website. February 16, 2015. http://www.kanjoya.com/measuring-impact-workplace-diversity-employee-perspective/.

20. Merriam-Wesbter.com, *s.v.* "Risk-taking."

21. *Merriam-Webster's Collegiate Dictionary,* 11th ed. *s.v.* "Innovation."

22. BusinessDictionary.com, *s.v.* "Entrepreneurship."

23. Dyer, Frank Lewis, and Thomas Commerford. *Edison: His Life and Inventions.* Volume 2. New York: Harper & Bros., 1910.

24. Hess, Edward D. *Learn or Die: Using Science to Build a Leading-Edge Learning Organization.* New York: Columbia University Press, 2014.

Chapter 4

SETTING THE STAGE FOR GREAT PERFORMANCE

Employees who believe that management is concerned about them as a whole person—not just an employee—are more productive, more satisfied, more fulfilled. Satisfied employees mean satisfied customers, which leads to profitability.

—Anne M. Mulcahy[1]

Whoever first coined the saying "Employees join companies and leave managers" certainly hit the nail on the head—and it's more true today than ever before for employees of *all* ages. The employees most likely to jump ship are (perhaps not surprisingly) members of the Millennial generation.

According to a 2014 report from the Bureau of Labor Statistics, employees between the ages of 25 and 34 years old have a median job tenure of 3 years (down from 3.2 years in 2012). This isn't an issue among only your youngest employees, though: the median tenure for *all* workers is a mere 4.6 years. On the bright side, older employees tend to stick around a lot longer:

> For example, the median tenure of workers ages 55 to 64 (10.4 years) was more than three times that of workers ages 25 to 34 years (3.0 years). A larger proportion of older workers than younger workers had 10 years or more of tenure. Among workers ages 60 to 64, 58 percent were employed for at least 10 years with their current employer in January 2014, compared with only 12 percent of those ages 30 to 34.[2]

The results of a 2016 CareerBuilder study support the belief that employees have one eye on the door: "76 percent of full-time employed workers are either actively looking for or open to new job opportunities."[3] In an earlier CareerBuilder study, 69 percent of respondents indicated that searching for new opportunities was a part of their "regular daily routine," with 30 percent of them actively looking every week.[4] And such lack of loyalty hurts business. In a survey of executives and managers by the American Management Association, 33 percent of respondents felt that "employee loyalty has a direct relationship to profits" and that a lack of loyalty has extremely negative consequences on employees' relationships with each other and with the organization.[5]

These studies (and many others like them) demonstrate why it's critical for managers to increase their leadership acumen in order to reduce employee job hopping and improve employee engagement and loyalty. The price of turnover can be extraordinarily high for organizations: one expert writes, "For entry-level employees, it costs between 30 percent and 50 percent of their annual salary to replace them," adding that the cost goes up (to 400 percent of annual salary) for top-level employees.[6] A constant revolving door of employees hurts you as a manager, because you must devote more of your time for training and because excessive turnover can leave senior executives questioning your ability to manage and lead others.

How can you reduce the flight risk of your employees? For starters, think about the managers you admire from your own experiences (whether in school or in a work environment). What traits made them great? Although each person will answer that question differently based on his or her situation, most responses to that question will highlight a manager's ability to inspire through the following actions:

1. Painting a crystal-clear picture of what performance is required and what goals need to be achieved
2. Providing feedback and coaching that help improve performance and achieve the objectives
3. Offering recognition and rewards when goals are met

This deceptively simple three-step formula is the foundation of great management and the key to getting the best performance from employees of all ages. If you do not perform these steps well, it's highly unlikely that you'll be able to tackle more advanced management skills, such as motivating four generations to work effectively together in the office. And if part of your structure for goal setting, giving feedback, and distributing rewards doesn't focus on multigenerational cooperation, you may end up pushing employees out the door. Because this formula is so critical for managing employees, it's worth taking a closer look at each step.

GOAL SETTING

Before you can motivate and engage your employees, you need to tell them what you expect of them. And be wary of assuming that, because of their work experience, older employees are already great at goal setting. There's a good chance they (along with younger colleagues) haven't really learned how to do this. Even though a strong correlation exists between a successful company, an effective goal-setting process, and the employees' actual performance, many organizations rush through formal goal setting (or overlook this process altogether).[7]

Employees who feel more connected to the company have greater motivation to help the organization achieve its goals than employees who have less of a connection and perhaps feel more like cogs in a wheel. Involving *all* employees (not just those in management) in the goal-setting process ensures that all are focused on how they can personally contribute to the company's success. As you start the goal-setting process, keep in mind that each generation will have its own ideas on how best to do this.

- Because Baby Boomers have been in the workforce longer than other generations, they may (depending on the positions they've held) have more strategic (and tactical) experience than their younger colleagues. Boomers prefer for managers to define the expected results and then give them the flexibility to figure out how to accomplish the goals as they see fit. Boomers are *great* with long-term goals and typically don't require many check-ins along the way (although that doesn't mean you should "dump and run").

- Generation Xers are also very independent. Like Boomers, they appreciate having their managers outline the expected results and then let them figure out how to accomplish them. More so than other generations, they prefer to work independently once goals have been established. (So set 'em up—then get out of their way!) Unlike other groups, though, Generation Xers often benefit from having short-term goals on the way to a big goal. With their hypercompetitive nature, the members of Generation X thrive on frequent recognition (say, quarterly rather than just annually).

- Millennials, on the other hand, have always been part of a team. Their whole lives, they have been surrounded by parents, grandparents, teachers, tutors, coaches, guidance counselors, and other adults who have either made decisions for them or given them strong guidance through the decision-making process. Accustomed to receiving participation awards and constant feedback, Millennials expect more recognition (even just a "Good job!" will do) than other generations. Because they live their lives online, they're used to having everything out in the open and externally validated by groups; consequently, they need more support than previous generations. More so than other generations, Millennials also expect their work goals to help them succeed with their personal goals (they see them as intertwined), so be prepared to help them make that connection. Unlike their predecessors, Millennials need and expect frequent check-ins and lots of feedback.

- The members of Generation Z are only just starting to enter the job market, and the full impact of their presence there won't be known for a while. But they are likely to share many of the expectations and motivations of the Millennials.

Getting Started

How you establish goals with your employees is just as important as drafting them in general. Your employees' commitment will be much greater if you involve them in the goal-setting process rather than merely hand them a list of goals and send them on their way. But what does "involve them" actually mean in practice?

As the leader, you define the expected results, then give your employees the freedom and autonomy to decide *how* to reach the end goal that you've articulated. Giving employees an active role in determining their own actions will greatly increase their motivation. Think about it: if your boss told you to complete a project, then defined exactly how to do it, do you think you'd feel particularly motivated? Under those circumstances, the project would likely feel much more like a task list than something that needs your brainpower and expertise. Sure, you'd probably get it done (because you place a high value on personal accountability). But your enthusiasm (and therefore your attention to detail and commitment level) for this project wouldn't be nearly as great as what you'd feel for the projects you own when you're in charge of the whole process.

One incredibly effective strategy I use when starting the goal-setting process is to partner my more experienced Baby Boomer and Generation X employees with Millennial employees. Such pairings promote team building, intergenerational cooperation, and understanding of each generation's value and contributions. Before the pairs go off to work on their goals, however, I explain that *everyone* is expected to share his or her goals and discuss the others' goals. So the older generations aren't just advising the younger generations—the Millennials are expected to give their thoughts on the goals of their Generation X and Baby Boomer colleagues, too. Such reverse mentoring ensures that the organization isn't just engaging in business as usual but tackling problems and goals from a fresh perspective each time. This new approach can be a bit bumpy in the beginning, and you'll need to ensure that everyone is listening to one another. But making a point to include all voices in your team meetings about goals will demonstrate to employees that *everyone* matters. Remember, you can't just *say* that you're an inclusive manager: you need to lead in a way that *shows* that you're an inclusive manager.

I've also found it quite useful to assign every employee the individual goal of promoting intergenerational cooperation in the department. When I ask,

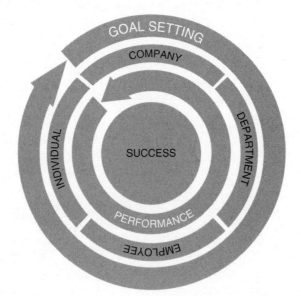

"How will you personally contribute to the successful operation of the department as a team?" I am always amazed by the many powerful ideas that my employees come up with. Their responses also help me identify anyone who is struggling to achieve that goal and who might need more direct help in making the adjustment to having older or younger coworkers. Additionally, adding "promote internal cooperation" as an individual goal (and one that gets discussed during performance reviews) underscores the priority placed on having all generations get along. If you want employees to take employee inclusion seriously, then they need to be evaluated on how they accomplish—or fail to accomplish—this. Without consequences, you're just giving it lip service.

What if your company *doesn't* have published goals and objectives? First, if you're in human resources or management, push your executive team to establish goals. Use the preceding diagram to bolster your argument that employee performance plays a strong role in the company's ability to achieve its goals. Be sure to point out that when the company lacks goals, any work being done might not support (and might even undermine!) senior management's priorities.

Second, if your company lacks goals and your management team is slow to establish them, don't let that stop you from creating your own department goals. (Your Millennial and Generation Z employees will *demand* them.) Use your company's mission statement or founding principles as the basis for department and individual goals. Pretty much all companies have a mission that includes selling their services and products to consumers or other businesses, so at the very least the goals for your department (and corresponding individual goals) can address how to help the company achieve those sales. If your organization isn't well established yet, don't worry: it's not unusual for new companies to lack detailed specific goals beyond selling their services and products. In fact, at Oxygen we didn't establish formal company goals until four years in. Right from the beginning, though, my employees always had individual goals that supported helping the company sell our services and spend efficiently.

Getting SMART

After creating your department goals, communicate them to your manager (and HR) and get his or her buy-in. Soliciting that input demonstrates your superior management skills and might even inspire senior management to get its act together and create goals for the entire company. Once you obtain any required approvals (or, at the minimum, acknowledgment of your efforts), your next step is to SMARTify those goals.

Applying SMART criteria (first detailed by management consultant George Doran) to an employee goal not only makes it possible to determine when the goal is successfully completed but also allows for specific feedback on an employee's performance (which is critical for the reward phase).[8] The words represented by the SMART acronym have varied slightly over time (and according to who's using them), but here's the version most widely used today:

- Specific—identifiable and observable
- Measurable—objectively quantifiable
- Achievable—moderately difficult, but realistic
- Relevant—meaningful to the individual, department, and organization
- Time-bound—completable within a specific time

As a manager, you play a key role in your employees' successes—and in their failures. To avoid the latter, position your team for success by establishing SMART goals and objectives that are clearly in line with the company's path to success. And be aware that all employees may need help with SMARTifying goals (and, as discussed in the previous section, with creating goals in general), because this process is likely to be new to them—even to employees who have been in the workforce for a while.

EVALUATING EMPLOYEE PERFORMANCE

To reiterate: before you can give effective feedback to your employees, you must define goals for them. In the absence of well-crafted goals, feedback is meaningless because without the context that goals provide, it cannot distinguish good behavior from bad and cannot provide clear direction on how to improve performance. So your first step toward becoming a successful manager of employees of any age is to create SMART goals. Once those are in place, you'll be able to improve your employees' performance through feedback and coaching. Many people use those terms interchangeably, but the two practices are actually very different from each other. Feedback focuses on past behavior and is instructional (i.e., you're telling the employee how tasks should have been completed or how performance should improve). Coaching, on the other hand, focuses on future behavior, is advice oriented, and aims to help an employee discover— and unlock—his or her performance potential.

Before examining each concept in detail, it's important to review each generation's expectations for coaching and feedback:

- *Baby Boomers:* This generation was raised in a working environment in which very little, if any, feedback was provided (and coaching was pretty much out of the question). From a manager's perspective that could be a good thing, because Boomer employees don't have high expectations. You may be surprised, however, to see employees of this generation blossom through effective coaching. Managers need to tread carefully with this group, though: because Baby Boomers generally prefer to figure things out on their own, it's important not to micromanage them.

- *Generation X:* Coming of age in the wake of corporate downsizing and economic downturns, this group of employees is fairly distrustful and wary of management. Help mitigate those feelings of angst by providing feedback and coaching to this group at regular intervals. Just as they benefit from having short-term goals (as part of a larger project), Generation Xers also benefit from regular (and more frequent) feedback and coaching, which together can help you win their loyalty.
- *Millennials and Generation Z:* Both of these generations require more frequent updates and feedback (daily, or at least weekly) than their predecessors, and they expect their managers' support and involvement to help them achieve their goals. The members of these generations won't allow managers to take a hands-off approach and will actively seek your guidance if you don't offer it. One sign that your Millennial is disengaged is if he or she stops asking for your feedback—an indication that he or she is about to leave for the next opportunity. Both Millennial and Generation Z employees need short-term goals, and they both expect to be rewarded when they meet your expectations. Rewards can be small (as little as a "Great job!" can suffice), but even that little bit will go a long way toward making them feel secure in their decision to stay with you as their manager.

My management style is fairly direct: rather than guess how much feedback or coaching employees want, I *ask* them how much they want—on both the project level (e.g., "Do you need more frequent check-ins to give me the number of updates I need?") and on their personal goals. Providing feedback and coaching isn't a task you should carry out on your own. For those processes to be effective, you have to work with your employees on them. By involving your employees, you make sure they have as much (if not more) ownership of their success and career development as you do.

Effective Feedback

A 2009 survey by Leadership IQ found that employees of all ages crave feedback now more than ever—yet they aren't getting it: two-thirds of respondents get "too little interaction with their boss[es]," and over one-half of them say they don't get enough "positive feedback" or "constructive criticism" from them. Employees who are unhappy in this regard are "43 percent less likely to recommend their company to others" as "great" workplaces.[9] Clearly, employers who want their employees to stick around need to work hard to make them happy. And making them happy means giving them the feedback they need.

Giving effective feedback entails taking responsibility for the whole communication cycle—being *clear* on your expectations and ensuring that your employee *understands* what you're asking him or her to do. Employees of all ages can benefit from feedback, so although Millennial and Generation Z employees will *demand* it, don't neglect more experienced workers (who may not be clamoring for feedback, but can definitely use it). It's a two-way process, because both parties are working to find common ground on expectations and performance. Good feedback can mean the difference between a motivated (and accountable) worker and one who's merely showing up and punching a clock (or looking for employment elsewhere).

Feedback is particularly beneficial for reducing uncertainty, solving problems, and improving the quality of an employee's work product. When given properly, it can strengthen the relationship between a manager and her or his direct reports by creating an environment of trust. In such an environment, failures and mistakes are considered opportunities to learn and improve performance—and not as opportunities to berate an employee. Most importantly, feedback can and should be given not just when employees need improvement but also when their performance is great. Remember, the point of feedback is to correct past problems in an effort to change the future behavior of your employee. So by giving feedback when the employee is doing well, you're encouraging more positive performance in the future.

It's important to understand the difference between ineffective feedback and effective feedback. Feedback is *not* effective if it:

- Judges individuals, not actions. (There's a big difference between saying, "You're late" and saying, "You clearly don't care about your job because you're late every day.")
- Speaks for others. (It should draw on your own observations, not on information obtained via other parties.)
- Ping-pongs between negative and positive messages. (Many first-time managers are uncomfortable delivering a negative message, so they will quickly balance it with a positive comment. This can undermine the value of the feedback, though. The point of delivering negative feedback is to talk about what performance you want. So fully discuss your expectations for future behavior—*then* discuss what the employee is doing well.)
- Goes on too long. (Make your point, then move on.)
- Contains an implied threat. (If the employee's job is on the line, state so directly—don't imply it.)
- Uses inappropriate humor. (Inexperienced managers may try to lighten the mood by cracking a joke or saying that the employee's behavior was "not as bad as So-and-so's." Giving negative feedback is a serious matter—and your delivery should reflect that.)
- Is a question, not a statement. (Don't ask, "Do you think you did a good job?" Rather, state where you want to see improvement. After all, employees rarely think they did a bad job.)
- Is general and vague. (Feedback should be as specific as your SMART goals. General feedback gets a general response—but specific feedback can actually change performance.)

To be effective, feedback to employees must establish clear expectations and outcomes by being both actionable and objective. It must:

- Be specific. (It is based on objective firsthand experience and observation of job performance.)
- Identify the action or behavior. (It constructively, clearly, and specifically describes the action or behavior for which feedback is being provided.)
- Describe what did or didn't work. (It cites specific examples of how the individual was or was not completely effective in certain instances.)
- Suggest what should be done differently. (It presents an alternative way of acting or behaving that would result in improved performance.)
- Provide an acceptable benefit. (It pinpoints an area in which you and the recipient believe improvement would benefit her or him, the department, and the company.)
- Be followed up on. (Progress toward improvement must be tracked. After all, feedback without follow-up wastes both your time and your employees' time because it sends a clear signal that you don't actually care about improvement.)

As you work to include these characteristics in your feedback, keep in mind that effective feedback isn't just about you talking while the employee listens—it's two-way communication. You must actively listen to your employees and pay attention to both the content (the *what*) and the intent (the *why*) of their messages. As your employees describe their reasoning behind their actions, confirm your understanding by periodically summarizing what you've heard. Ask probing questions that can help you get to the heart of any challenges your employees might be facing in completing a task (and enable you to help them make the right decision next time). Also, pay attention to nonverbal communication (part of how the message is conveyed). As you listen, be empathetic and nonjudgmental. Do what you can to convey "We're in this together" rather than "I'm the all-knowing manager, and you're doing a terrible job."

When it is your time to speak, be honest, not threatening. Remember that effective feedback doesn't focus on dishing out criticism; rather, it identifies solutions to help your employees achieve tasks. Occasionally, an employee's performance might require a critical discussion that kicks off the termination process; in general, though, feedback is best used to generate options for creating and nurturing employee ownership, accountability, and (ultimately) improvements in employee performance.

Effective Coaching

Coaching can be one of the most rewarding aspects of being a manager. When done correctly, it can have a tremendously transformative impact on your employees and help them achieve more than even they thought they could! Effective coaching can have a transformative impact on managers, too. The lives I touched through my coaching efforts are what I remember best from the more than two decades I spent in corporate America.

What is coaching and how does it differ from feedback? Whereas feedback focuses on examining past behavior to identify areas of improvement (and therefore affect future performance), coaching develops an employee's knowledge and skill sets and expands your employee's viewpoint about his or her abilities.

Whether formal or informal, coaching is an ongoing dialogue with employees about their strategic development and how to tackle projects beyond their present capabilities. Although any moment can be an opportunity to help your employee improve his or her skills, coaching works best as a normal part of your daily or weekly conversation with an employee. (I've also found it useful to hold bimonthly meetings with my employees specifically focused on coaching and developing.) As with feedback, all employees have goals—and all of them can benefit from coaching. Just because Millennials and Generation Z employees expect coaching conversations to help them achieve their goals doesn't mean you should focus only on those workers, though. Be sure to spend time with Generation X and Baby Boomer employees, too, to help them continue to grow and expand their knowledge and skill sets.

Current projects provide a great framework for starting a coaching conversation. Instead of the typical status update, a coaching conversation addresses the project in the context of future growth. Here are some questions that can launch a coaching conversation:

- What experience and knowledge gained in your last project will help you tackle your next project?
- Going forward, what hurdles will you be on the lookout for?
- What new skills did you acquire on your last project?
- What was challenging about that project? What was easy?
- What lessons did you learn from that project? What lessons would you recommend disseminating to the entire department?
- What options did you consider for addressing problems or concerns with that project? Now that the project is finished, would you make the same decisions? Why or why not?
- How does completing this goal get you closer to your personal goals?
- Thinking about your career, what aspects of your last project would you like to do more of in your day-to-day work?
- How does your work help the company achieve its goals?

If I'm having a coaching conversation about a hurdle on a specific project (and not specifically on the employee's career development), I focus on questions designed to get the employee to think outside the box for solutions (rather than wait for me to outline next steps). If I'm coaching an employee about issues she or he is having with a coworker, I focus my questions on how my employee might be contributing to the problem—and what changes in himself or herself can improve the situation. By asking questions, my goal is to help employees transcend their current approaches and expand their strategic thinking and problem-solving abilities.

Coaching is effective if it:

- Provides encouragement and challenges the employee's current thinking. (The conversation is rooted in support but also seeks to push employees out of their comfort zones.)
- Involves active listening. (Don't stop at the stated facts. As a manager you must seek the *why* behind an employee's actions and thoughts.)
- Asks powerful questions. (This is key to getting to the root of an issue so your employees can figure out their next steps without you telling them how to proceed.)
- Provides a different lens. (Sharing perspectives highlights differences that can be instructive and lead to a wider range of options.)
- Creates ownership and accountability. (Both sides should be invested in the coaching.)

There are many ways to conduct a coaching session. For example, some people want very structured guidance, whereas others prefer a more informal approach. Regardless of your particular style, coaching should be designed to help your employees grow, and with that aim in mind I find the well-known GROW model for problem solving and goal setting to be especially helpful.[10] Use this model to frame the steps of your coaching process:

- Goal—Define the short-term goals of each coaching session and how they support the long-term objective.
  - ☐ What do we want to achieve in this session?
  - ☐ What's the long-term objective, and how does this session help you get closer to fulfilling it?
- Reality—Understand where the employee stands in his or her ability to complete the tasks relevant to the current project.
  - ☐ What's the current status of the project?
  - ☐ What have you done so far?
  - ☐ Who or what is involved?
- Options—Empower employees to come up with other options or new possibilities that they might not have envisioned. (You may have to step in and offer assistance, but your goal is to help employees come up with solutions on their own so that they are actively thinking of—and learning—new ways to approach problem solving.)
  - ☐ What can you do?
  - ☐ What options are available?
  - ☐ How can you come up with new options?

- Will—Have the employee identify next steps based on the new options you've helped him or her uncover.
  - ☐ What will you do?
  - ☐ When will you do it?
  - ☐ What help do you need?

Interestingly, you won't need to make many adjustments to this version of GROW-based coaching when using it with employees of varying experience levels. These questions work equally well with both less experienced and more experienced employees, and this technique can be applied repeatedly to any project. As employees continue to expand their skill sets, they also increase their ability to come up with options for solving problems as well.

When I use GROW-based coaching to develop softer skills (such as leadership acumen in senior employees), I often augment it with additional learning opportunities through book recommendations, training opportunities, or even interviews with other senior leaders in the company. As you look to expand your employee's thinking, remember not to limit your own thinking! Adjust the questions as needed to develop increasingly complex skills or to incorporate future strategies that help increase an employees' critical reasoning and problem-solving abilities. As you expand your own management toolkit, remember that practice makes perfect: the more you work on delivering effective coaching, the better you'll be at it.

YOU GET WHAT YOU REWARD

Once you've established a clear baseline of expectations, managers can be ready to reward and recognize superior performance when it occurs. Why should senior leaders take an interest in their companies' recognition and rewards programs? Because the old adage "You get what you reward" rings especially true in the business world.

It almost goes without saying that everyone likes to receive recognition and rewards. Unfortunately, however, managers often underestimate their value. A 2012 survey of over 800 organizations by Bersin & Associates (now Bersin by Deloitte) highlighted how critical it is for companies to offer recognition and rewards programs. For example, companies with such programs see both significant improvements in their employees' work and dramatic decreases in voluntary employee turnover. Perhaps most significantly three out of four companies have a recognition program, but only 58 percent of employees believe their organizations have these programs. This disconnect indicates that despite the money organizations invest in recognition programs—about 1 percent of payroll—many employees do not even know their programs exist.

So how can we reward our employees in ways that actually motivate and engage them? And do expectations (and definitions) of rewards change as individuals (both employees and managers) gain more experience in the workforce?

Before developing specific strategies for rewards, consider these key factors regarding motivation:

- *Motivation is personal.* Each and every employee has his or her own expectations and understandings of what constitutes a reward. Therefore, a one-size-fits-all approach to recognition and rewards won't cut it.
- *Motivation is not a constant.* What motivates an employee changes over time. Whether you're rolling out a formal recognition plan now or have an existing program, you must review your recognition plan annually to make sure it meets your employees' needs and hasn't gone stale. Organizations—and people—change all the time, so think of supporting employee motivation as a process and not as a one-time task.
- *Motivation is intrinsic.* For all this talk about motivation, when it comes right down to it your employees are the only ones who can truly motivate themselves. You can't do it for them. But you *can* set an example and create a motivating environment—that is, an atmosphere conducive to success.
- *Motivating employees starts with motivating yourself.* Interestingly, when you hate your job, it seems as though all of your team members hate theirs, too. When your employees see that you are stressed out, the chances are good that they will be stressed out as well. Just as negativity is contagious, so, too, is enthusiasm. When you're excited and motivated about your job, it's much easier for those around you to feel the same about theirs.

It's important to note that recognition is not about spending more (whether money or time) but about spending smarter. Recognition that actually matters to the employee will be more motivating and effective, particularly in the long run. As discussed in the previous chapter, having a yearly conversation with each employee about his or her long-term goals (and how those goals may have changed) can help you identify rewards that connect with intrinsic motivations and are far more effective (and enduring) than those rewards based on external factors (such as money).

SENIOR LEADERSHIP VERSUS PEER-TO-PEER RECOGNITION

Management's job is to define the company's mission and strategic plans. But managers can't just issue decrees and expect employees to excel at executing them. Leaders need to find ways to reinforce what is valued (or even required), and recognition is one key solution. By tying individual employee goals to department goals (which, in turn, are tied to company goals), rewarding and recognizing individual performance ultimately help the company achieve success.

In departments of all sizes, no matter how far removed they are from the CEO's office, the manager's job is to define the mission and goals of his or her department, then reward employees who successfully accomplish those goals.

Recognition efforts can also increase your employees' motivation to help the company achieve its objectives. Like personal accountability, motivation in the work environment manifests as an employee's enthusiasm about and internal drive to accomplish his or her assigned goals. So the more motivated an employee is, the more likely he or she is to put forth his or her best effort on behalf of the company.

HR managers have long operated under the mistaken belief that recognition from company leadership carries the most weight among workers. But employees actually tend to place a much higher value on recognition from their peers. Why? For starters, peers know what each other is doing on a day-to-day basis, so a "Thank you" or a "Well done!" from colleagues can carry much more meaning than one from someone who does completely different work in a completely different context. Peers also generally have the best understanding of what their fellow employees are actually working on (and its level of difficulty), making recognition from someone who knows (i.e., a respected colleague) more meaningful. Additionally, top-down recognition is often viewed as being connected to office politics or workplace social networks, and because the giver and the recipient usually have some distance (in work assignments, in authority, and even in terms of physical office locations) between them, this type of recognition rarely reaches the company's quiet—but critical—high performers.

To counter some of the negative associations with top-down recognition, some businesses have adopted peer-to-peer recognition programs that let anyone in the company publicly acknowledge someone else's achievements. Although such social-oriented programs are fairly new (but rapidly growing in popularity), these forms of recognition actually aren't much different from the certificates or trophies that companies have been awarding to employees for years. Instead of displaying items on their cubicle walls or desks, however, recipients can now see their recognition publicly displayed on leader boards or on the company website, for example.

Peer-to-peer recognition can take many forms. The online retailing giant Zappos has come up with many innovations in this area. For example, one program enables employees to reward coworkers with Zappos dollars (Zollars) that can be spent on Zappos-branded items, traded in for movie tickets, or converted into charitable donations. Employees have the option to reward each other with *real* dollars, too: through the Coworker Bonus Program, employees can each give $50 a month to another employee who goes above and beyond his or her regular responsibilities. (Notably, managers cannot receive money from or give it to their direct reports.) Such recognition programs have been enormously successful at Zappos (when I toured the company's headquarters, every employee I met praised them), but that doesn't mean all companies need to replicate those same strategies. However a company recognizes its employees—and whether that recognition takes place in weekly department conference calls, in monthly company-wide town hall meetings, or in another setting—having a good peer-based program in place can help any organization improve employee motivation.

THE BASICS OF RECOGNITION

Basic forms of recognition are those that address the *physiological/survival* and *safety* elements of Maslow's hierarchy of needs. In this category, the main drivers for employees of all ages include the following:

- *Salary commensurate with position:* Money *is* a contender in motivation— but many managers erroneously think that money is the *only* thing their employees want. Granted, if an employee isn't earning enough—or is earning just enough—to cover basic needs (rent, food, etc.), then salary will play a greater role in motivating that individual. For proof of this, just look at the high turnover in low-paying hourly positions: those employees are more apt to leave such jobs if doing so means earning as little as 25 cents more an hour, because even small changes at that pay scale can make a big difference to people struggling to meet their basic needs. That said, once those basic needs are met, money has less influence as a motivational tool (for example, among seniors who've amassed healthy savings, Millennials and Generation Z employees who can rely on parental support, or Generation X employees who live in dual-income households). Keep in mind, too, that high-performing employees of all ages are likely targets for poaching by your competitors—and if those other companies have better recognition programs than yours, your employees may not stick around. Yes, you can and should offer raises, but it's tough to sustain employee motivation over the long run if the workplace lacks motivation-driving elements beyond salary.
- *Job security:* Fear of losing a job can demotivate employees of any age. Even workers who have enough financial security so that the paycheck itself isn't their top priority for working (such as seniors who opt to stay in the workforce for continued connection and mental stimulation) can experience a great deal of stress if they constantly feel that their jobs are on the chopping block. While consulting for numerous companies in the midst of broad organizational changes, I've seen firsthand how common it is for employees to disengage when they're worried about their financial future. And not only can job instability decrease engagement, but it can also keep employees constantly looking elsewhere for opportunities with more job security.
- *Understanding in a personal crisis:* In any workplace and with any employee, sometimes life just happens. When employers understand that problems arise outside the office and are willing to work with employees in times of a crisis, that can go a long way toward building the goodwill that's

key to securing an employee for a longer tenure. For example, one of my direct reports at Oxygen was barely able to hold it together during those first few months after he had twins. Thanks to stress and sleep deprivation, his work suffered. Up to this point, his performance had been outstanding, and I knew he was going through a rough patch. So instead of punishing him, I eased up a bit on assigning projects to him. He was able to catch his breath, and after four months his performance sprang back stronger than ever! Because I helped him through his difficult period, once it passed he was even *more* committed to me and to the company.

INTRINSIC MOTIVATORS

As previously mentioned, motivation that comes from within an individual has a more lasting effect on that person than external rewards (such as money, titles, corner offices, etc.), whose positive effects soon fade. Here are some strategies for helping employees develop intrinsic motivation.

- *Keep employees in the know.* No one enjoys feeling like a cog in a wheel. Employees are more engaged in their work and with the company if they have a sense of the big picture, not just their small slice of the company. So give them insight into how the company operates (and how it is doing financially). With this knowledge, employees are more likely to feel that the organization is *their* company, not merely a place where they work in accounting or HR or marketing.
- *Assign interesting and engaging work.* Management theorist Frederick Herzberg once said, "If you want someone to do a good job, give them a good job to do." So give your employees good jobs by making sure that their responsibilities include something of interest to them. Even in jobs that are inherently boring, having at least one or two stimulating projects can motivate employees to perform well in the mundane tasks, too.
- *Invite involvement and ownership in decisions.* Most companies don't prioritize involving employees in decisions that affect them. Perhaps it's time to reconsider that practice. Keeping employees in the loop is not only respectful (and makes them feel like part of the company), but it's also practical: people who are closest to a situation typically have the best insight on how to improve it. Employees on the ground floor of an issue often know what works (and what doesn't) and can provide valuable insight into how to resolve a problem quickly and effectively. In addition, employees who have a hand in crafting a solution feel ownership of it and are therefore more invested in working toward its successful implementation.
- *Increase visibility and opportunity.* Don't make assumptions (particularly any based on an employee's age) about how much visibility and opportunity your employees want. Through experience managing thousands of employees, I've found that everyone (regardless of age or position) likes to be recognized and noticed by more than just his or her supervisors after doing a good job. Whether or not they want promotions or more challenging

work (two things that are likely to be of more interest to Generation Xers, Millennials, and Generation Z employees than to Baby Boomers), all employees flourish when they receive more visible recognition and opportunities that are personally meaningful. At Oxygen, for example, I assigned a Baby Boomer employee to a task force that lay outside the scope of her day-to-day work but was still within her skill set. This employee placed a high value on her experiences with other companies prior to joining Oxygen, and she flourished in this new role. Being given this responsibility confirmed to her that her input still mattered—a belief that motivated her on all of her subsequent projects!

- *Provide autonomy.* Employees value the freedom to do their jobs as they see fit. So if your employees are able to get their jobs done (and done well) on their own, *leave them alone!* When you give high-performing employees more autonomy, you increase the likelihood that those employees will continue to perform as desired. Even with new recruits who haven't yet proven themselves in your company, you can provide autonomy in work assignments by telling those employees what needs to be done without dictating exactly how to do it.

- *Be loyal.* This can be a challenge for employers, but as a boss you should demonstrate loyalty to your employees. This can include being transparent (when possible), providing accurate feedback designed to improve the employee's performance, and giving credit to employees for their work (rather than taking credit for it yourself).

- *Show appreciation.* It's amazing how many managers don't thank their employees for completing tasks. Yes, it's their job to do that work, but why not take a moment to say a simple "Thank you"? Employees of all ages like to be appreciated (and Millennials in particular will be completely turned off—and looking for another employer—if they aren't), and whether appreciation takes the form of small gestures or big statements, it can go a long way toward motivating and retaining them.

- *Cultivate a fun environment.* It's common sense that when people like their workplaces, they're more likely to stay with their companies longer and put more energy into their work. (Millennials place an especially high value on having a fun workplace.) Even if your company is a more buttoned-up or formal environment, you can still try to inject some fun into it even at just the department level.

CAREER AND DEVELOPMENT RECOGNITION

When considering how to motivate your team, keep in mind that growth opportunities are a great option that in many instances doesn't require spending additional money. In fact, such opportunities can actually help a company's bottom line, because employees who believe they are continually expanding their skill sets and abilities are more likely to stick around longer. The moment the learning stops is the moment an employee starts looking for the next opportunity. So keep providing your employees with more challenging projects, even if they don't necessarily equate to different jobs. Growth opportunities can take many forms, such as lead-ing a team, being in charge of a project, or getting more exposure to senior-level executives. Talk with your employees about their long-term career and personal goals so you can tie career recognition opportunities to their interests. People are much more motivated to accomplish goals when they have a personal stake in them (and aren't just working to benefit the company).

As far as recognitions and rewards are concerned, one size definitely does *not* fit all, particularly in an age-diverse workplace. When managing workers of any age, it's important to understand their motivations and what rewards they value. While younger workers may be gunning to get that next big promotion as quickly as possible, older workers (more than other age groups) typically prioritize an environment in which they're valued and respected for their knowledge and expe-rience. Older workers often also value a more flexible work environment that requires fewer hours but includes more vacation time and maintains their bene-fits. (The latter is particularly important to employees near retirement who aren't yet eligible for Medicare.) Older workers aren't the only group who value flex-ibility, though. A 2015 report by EY, for example, found that Millennials (just as much as Generation Xers) value jobs that give them more flexibility and help them achieve greater work-life balance.[11] So if you want to know what rewards and recognition your employees value, you need to *ask* them!

That said, some reward strategies have very broad appeal across job functions, industries, and demographic groups (including different generations). With some tweaking, you can likely adjust some or all of these to suit your employees' needs. And rewarding and motivating employees don't necessarily have to break the company bank: all of the options below are low-cost or no-cost programs.

- Have your employee present his or her findings or project successes to senior management. This strategy is particularly effective for those seek-ing promotions, because it gives them an opportunity to show their chops to the bosses.
- Arrange for the employee to have lunch with a senior executive of his or her choice. (At Oxygen, outstanding employees got to have lunch with the CEO or COO, with the conversation focused on mentoring and coaching the employee—a simple yet powerful reward that was very popular.)
- Include the employee in your meetings with senior leaders to expose him or her to your responsibilities, then discuss the meeting afterward to find out what he or she learned from the experience.
- Have the employee expand his or her knowledge of the company by job shadowing another executive. (Don't limit this opportunity to young or junior employees: I've found it to be highly valued by employees of all ages. Even Baby Boomers who may be nearing retirement and aren't seeking for a promotion appreciate gaining insight into the senior-most workings of the company.)
- Send a note to the employee's home touting his or her accomplishments. This is particularly effective with Millennial and Generation Z employees, who often still live at home with parents who are involved in their work lives.

But Generation X and Baby Boomer employees respond just as positively when their bosses praise them to the employees' spouses or partners. (Who *doesn't* want close family members to know how great we are?)

- Encourage the employee to accept an assignment in another department. This isn't a transfer but a temporary arrangement based on discussions you have with the other department's leader to identify quantifiable projects that someone unfamiliar with the department could accomplish. For example, one of my assistants had an interest in public relations, so I arranged for her to spend approximately five hours a week helping the PR department prepare for a major company event. (She did a fantastic job for them while still keeping up with her existing duties.) Another employee who wanted to increase his financial acumen helped the executive who managed my department's budgets prepare the rolled-up financial statements every month. (This turned out to be terrific training for getting a better understanding of the department—so much so that I eventually required *all* of my employees to do this!)

- Arrange for employees to sit at the company-sponsored table at a fundraiser or other community event. Someone who isn't in sales or marketing (and therefore doesn't do this all the time) might really appreciate—and benefit from—the opportunity to get a different perspective on the company's outreach.

- Help your employee pursue leadership opportunities. Recommend your employee to the CEO's new task force, for example, or let him or her take the lead at your next staff meeting. Find out your employee's career aspirations, then identify assignments that will expand his or her skill set in the desired direction.

Millennial and Generation Z employees will expect their managers to provide these sorts of opportunities. But more seasoned employees will also welcome these opportunities to continue to develop their skills. The increased productivity you gain by providing interesting projects beyond day-to-day tasks will, by preventing jobs from becoming stale and helping people feel more motivated and engaged, more than compensate for the time your employees are away from their regular jobs.

Notice that rewarding an employee does not have to entail spending money. The key is to come up with rewards and recognition that have meaning and value to that particular employee. You can't come up with these ideas in a vacuum: you'll need to have a conversation with each employee about his or her goals. One of the biggest mistakes managers can make is thinking that they know all about their employees' preferences without actually *talking* with those employees. Each person has his or her own personal criteria for what makes a good reward, so be sure to discuss this with each employee annually (or even more often).

Not all rewards have to be career oriented, of course. For example, I've given employees movie passes and time off to go see a movie during the workday (a decadent treat that everyone appreciates!). Giving an employee some of his or her favorite candy or soda (after finding out what those are by actually asking the employee, not by guessing) is another simple and effective way to say "Thank you" (and one that won't break the bank). If you spend some time thinking about each of your employees, you'll discover plenty of recognition options — and the personal touch will help build their loyalty to you as their manager.

NOTES

1. Mulcahy, Anne M. Keynote address at Lifecare Inc's Life Event Management 2003 Conference. Rye Brook, New York, May 2003.

2. Bureau of Labor Statistics. "Employee Tenure in 2014." Bureau of Labor Statistics website. September 18, 2014. http://www.bls.gov/news.release/pdf/tenure.pdf.

3. CareerBuilder. "How to Rethink the Candidate Experience and Make Better Hires" CareerBuilder website. 2016. http://hiring.careerbuilder.com/promotions/candidatebehavior.

4. CareerBuilder. "2012 Candidate Behavior Study: The Myth of the Passive Job Seeker." CareerBuilder website. 2012. http://www.careerbuildercommunications.com/candidatebehavior2012/2012/.

5. American Management Association. "Survey Finds Employees Less Loyal Than Five Years Ago." American Management Association website. January 6, 2015. http://www.amanet.org/news/10606.aspx.

6. Borysenko, Karlyn. "What Was Management Thinking? The High Cost of Employee Turnover." EreMedia website. April 22, 2015. http://www.eremedia.com/tlnt/what-was-leadership-thinking-the-shockingly-high-cost-of-employee-turnover/.

7. Fitz-Enz, Jac, and Erik Breggern. "How Smart Human Capital Management Drives Financial Performance." SuccessFactors website. 2006. http://www.successfactors.com/en_us/lp/articles/smart-hcm.html.

8. Doran, George T. "There's a S.M.A.R.T. Way to Write Management's Goals and Objectives." *Management Review* 70, no. 11 (1981), 35–36.

9. Leadership IQ. "Study: Managers Making Recession Worse by Ignoring Workers." PRWeb website. December 2, 2009. http://www.prweb.com/releases/2009/12/prweb3285464.htm.

10. Unlike the framework for SMART goals, the GROW model didn't originate in one particular publication or speech. This model has been around for about three decades and has spread throughout management circles so widely and quickly that its original source has been lost. I've encountered versions of it in PowerPoint presentations, blog posts, conference talks, and many other management-related communication contexts.

11. EY. 2015. "Global Generations: A Global Study on Work-Life Challenges across Generations." www.ey.com/Publication/vwLUAssets/EY-global-generations-a-global-study-on-work-life-challenges-across-generations/$FILE/EY-global-generations-a-global-study-on-work-life-challenges-across-generations.pdf.

Chapter 5

BEING AN INCLUSIVE MANAGER

Creating and managing a diverse workforce is a process, not a destination.
  –R. Roosevelt Thomas Jr., *Beyond Race and Gender*[1]

In chapter 4, I discussed the importance of making diversity a business initiative, not just a "nice to have" program separate from corporate initiatives. When diversity is an organizational priority, it will actually get attention from senior management and won't be relegated to the back burner when resources are tight. Although having senior-level commitment is important, when it comes to valuing employees of all ages (and other diversity efforts), one cannot overlook the criticality of enlisting the individual managers in promoting an inclusive environment. It's easy for senior leaders to say all the right things, but if middle managers (who in essence run the organization) don't get on board, it will be tough for projects of any kind to succeed. After all, middle managers are the doers whose actions result in company goals being met. This group typically has *way* more interaction with a greater number of employees than the average CEO, who in most instances is outwardly facing. And as we know, "employees join companies and leave managers." Thus, the actions of middle managers in promoting an environment inclusive of all ages is even more critical than those at the senior-most levels.

THE BENEFITS OF INCLUSION

As part of my training practice, I lead a workshop entitled "Inspiring a Collaborative and Respectful Work Environment." During class, I have participants break up into groups and answer the following question:

> What are the benefits of a work environment in which diversity is valued, differences are respected, and staff members exhibit an inclusive behavior?

I typically hear a lot of the same answers from client to client, including greater creativity, better problem solving, more accurate reflections of customer and client bases, better representation of the population at large, and boosted morale. Other cited benefits include improved retention rates, increased productivity as team members work at their full potential, better customer relations, and reduction in employee complaints and grievances. Greater diversity can give a better understanding of those you work for, with, and around and can help for-profit companies enjoy greater profitability. These are all very compelling reasons to support diversity and inclusion, but as I point out to my workshop participants, chances are that each of them is probably being judged on a daily basis. For example, as soon as someone walks into a room, people make assumptions about that person based on his or her physical attributes. To underscore that point, I'll point to myself and say (with an appropriate sneer on my face):

- "Her suit's too dark and conservative for our company."
- "What's with her hair? It looks a little crazy and all over the place."
- "Why doesn't she have makeup on?" (Or "Boy, she has too much makeup on!").
- "Her voice is so deep … is she a man?"
- "She has a funny accent."

I then mention that I know these things are said about me because I've read them in anonymous responses to after-training surveys. When I ask participants how they would feel if someone said these things about them, participants typically respond with sincere outrage.

The goal of this exercise is to draw attention to the fact that at any moment, someone could be making judgments about each of us that have no tie-in to our ability to do the job. We've all been subjected to some age-based assumptions in the workplace at some point. We've been "too young" or "too old." Or maybe we were told we were "not hip enough" Or that the organization wanted "someone with more energy." Or perhaps we were passed over because the hiring manager didn't want to "hold someone's hand" but instead preferred "a person with more experience."

As some point in our professional lives, we've all been labeled without regard to our knowledge and abilities and only because someone made a snap decision based on our physical attributes and didn't even try to get to know us. The point of this workshop exercise is to point out that we all make these kinds of judgments—and we need to stop doing it.

BREAKING BAD HABITS

In his 2005 bestseller *Blink: The Power of Thinking Without Thinking*, Malcolm Gladwell wrote, "Our attitudes toward race, gender, and other diversity traits operate at two levels." First is the conscious, which means "what we choose to believe," and second is what happens on the unconscious level, which is our "immediate, automatic associations that tumble out before we've had time to think."[2] Such associations are a habit, something that we've done repeatedly, starting from when we were children (after all, our attitudes toward different cultures and people are based on our experiences growing up). The good news about habits is that with effort, you can turn them on their head. As the great historian Will Durant wrote (in his discussion of Aristotle's *Nichomachean Ethics*), "We are what we repeatedly do. Excellence, then, is not an act, but a habit."[3] To change your inner voice, start by becoming more aware of your thoughts when you first meet a person. What is the first association that goes through your mind? If it's negative, figure out what would be a better (and more realistic) association to have. Repeat that internal mantra each time you meet new people who share similar physical traits. To jump-start this process, stand on a busy street corner and as people walk by, practice running the new positive association through your mind. Verbalizing such associations can also help solidify them in your mind (although if you're talking to yourself on a street corner in some cities, a police officer may stop to check on you).

The key to breaking a bad habit is to notice when a negative thought goes through your mind about someone you meet and then immediately replace it with something positive. The more you practice awareness of your thoughts, the better control you will have over them, until soon the old habit has been replaced with far more productive thoughts. If controlling what pops into your mind sounds out of reach, consider Joyce Meyers's words in her book *Making Good Habits, Breaking Bad Habits*: "If you don't learn to control your thoughts, you will never learn how to control your behavior."[4]

FALSE THINKING OF NEW MANAGERS

New managers often believe that a promotion to a position of authority means they must now have all the answers. If that were only true! Experienced managers know that this just isn't the case—and recognize that they still have plenty of knowledge gaps and must keep learning each day.

If you're new to managing and aren't quite sure what to do, start by determining the value you bring to the group. Why did management put you in charge? Ask your boss, if he or she hasn't already answered this question. Ultimately, a manager's job is to set priorities and goals, then motivate employees of all ages to reach those goals. That doesn't mean you have to determine every goal for your department—far from it, actually. Tap into the knowledge base of your staff and enlist their help in determining what needs be accomplished in order to help the company meet its financial objectives. Push your staff (and yourself) to think outside the box and bring fresh ideas to the forefront. As Steve Jobs said, "A lot of times, people don't know what they want until you show it to them."[5] The same is true when leading a team: don't settle for business as usual but instead strive to solve problems that may not have been identified yet (but will eventually come to bite you). To accomplish this, however, a manager must be able to draw on the experiences of older employees and the new perspectives of younger recruits, and then blend them into a sound next step that everyone can get behind.

LEAD BY EXAMPLE

It's often pointed out that older employees want to be appreciated for their hard-earned knowledge, but in reality, *all* employees want that same respect. After all, younger employees have knowledge as well; it's just different from that of those who have been in the workforce longer. As a manager, part of your responsibility is to ensure that everyone values the differences each person brings into the workplace. That means ensuring respect by all employees to all employees. You can lead by example simply by demonstrating your own belief that generations should be treated fairly. If the office atmosphere requires you to try more persuasive tactics, consider shaking up the hierarchy and bucking everyone's expectations: assign a Baby Boomer to a social media project, for example, or ask a Millennial to lead a meeting. Your actions will send a strong message, so make it a point not to refer to individuals by their generation. Instead of framing an employee's desire to be promoted as a Millennial sense of entitlement, for example, recognize that everyone wants to progress in his or her career (and remember that you, too, once hoped to move up the corporate ladder quickly).

Continually remind yourself and your staff to focus more on generational similarities—of which there are many—rather than on differences. "There is no evidence that 35-year-old managers today are any different from 35-year-old managers a generation ago," says management expert Peter Cappelli, professor of management at the Wharton School and coauthor of *Managing the Older Worker*.[6] At heart, everyone wants the same things: a pleasant work environment, proper compensation, and recognition for a job well done. Acknowledging these similarities among the diverse members of your team will help you perceive them more as a cohesive group than as a disparate mix of generations.

DON'T EMULATE BAD MANAGERS

Without respect in the workplace, managers typically won't get the best out of their employees because they'll be more worried about promoting themselves rather than working as a cohesive team to solve problems. And if senior leaders exhibit those same behaviors, chances are slim that the company will perform at its best because department "silos" will focus on their own interests rather than on the company's success. In those instances, don't be surprised if the company experiences much higher turnover and fails to achieve its financial goals.

Unfortunately, there is little you can do as a middle manager if your senior leaders are awful at showing respect and valuing old and young alike. That said, it's important to understand that although you can't control what someone else does, you *can* control your own thoughts and actions. If you lead by example, your employees are more likely to follow suit—and the bad behavior can stop with you.

PROMOTING RESPECT

As a manager, one of your main jobs (if not your *primary* responsibility) is to unite and motivate your employees behind common goals. When that is accomplished, the power of experience combined with the boldness of new thinking can be a powerful recipe for getting things done *and* for future innovation. To promote respect among your team:

- *Think before you speak.* As a manager, your words have the power to motivate or squash someone's enthusiasm. Acknowledge the other person's thoughts, even if the answer is no.
- *Encourage diverse opinions.* Nothing is worse than having everyone agree to a plan of action in a meeting and then hear someone say afterward that he or she didn't actually like the plan. Create an environment in which diverse opinions are welcome.
- *Manage conflict in a constructive manner.* Conflict happens in the best of departments and organizations any time two people have different ideas on how to accomplish a task. Don't give in to frustration and lose control in an angry outburst. Instead, view conflict as an opportunity to hear different (possibly better) ideas on how to solve a problem.
- *Don't dismiss jobs you consider "beneath you" in the organizational hierarchy.* In a recent workshop I conducted on inclusion, a woman was about to provide input on respecting others when a young man approached with a microphone (we were in a large theater). She summarily dismissed him with a wave of her hand and a dirty look before saying, "I don't need that." It took all my self-control to not point out to the woman that she had just disrespected someone who was just doing his job. Remember, everyone's job is important, even if it doesn't seem important to you.
- *Don't engage in gossip or negative conversations about your organization.* Once you become a manager, you represent your company, both in the office and outside. Gossip is rarely positive and works to break down respect for other employees and your company. If you truly don't like your company, perhaps it's time to look elsewhere.
- *Rely on facts, not on suppositions.* It's easy to make assumptions about what people mean when they say something, particularly if it's via text or e-mail (where tone is *very* difficult to ascertain). Before acting on what you *think* someone means, ask that person what he or she actually intends.
- *Problems come and go every day.* Solutions need to meet the greater needs of the organization, not just your department. The manager's job is to solve today's problems while also keeping in mind the bigger picture. Don't forget that, even in the heat of the moment.
- *Ask employees how they want to be treated.* Once again, don't make assumptions (remember what people say about the word *assume* …). Don't shy away from your differences (particularly if you and your employees are from different generations); instead, tactfully discuss how you can come together to accomplish what needs to get done.
- *Eliminate stereotypes and other negative generalizations.* As I discussed at length in chapter 3, each generation has many misconceptions about the others. Instead of letting those misperceptions drive a wedge between the

various ages, address differences in a constructive manner and treat them as learning opportunities for all involved.

- *Be a stellar communicator.* Understanding differences (of any kind) isn't enough to make them go away. As linguist Deborah Tannen writes in *You Just Don't Understand*, "the person who understands how difference causes communication to break down can take the initiative to try and make the communication work."[7] Use your words and influence to bridge the communication gap between others in the organization.
- *Be a role model.* To *get* respect, you have to *give* respect. So be a role model of respect throughout the organization and aspire to be one of the managers with whom employees want to work for years to come (even as you continue to move up the corporate ladder).

INNOVATION AT BOTH ENDS OF THE SPECTRUM

Today, many of the startups and younger companies that are actively recruiting don't even look at resumes of older candidates, thinking they won't fit into the corporate culture or are too stuck in their ways to bring any new ideas to the table. Not only is this an inaccurate assumption, but these companies are only hurting themselves by preventing the workplace from being more diverse and staffed with seasoned professionals. Fear of change and fear of ideas and people who are different in the workplace are counterproductive. Just because a company is new or uses a new technology doesn't mean it can't benefit from the wisdom of industry veterans.

And there are a number of older entrepreneurial minds out there. A 2014 *Business Insider* article reported that one in three new US businesses was started by someone over 50.[8] This isn't a new trend, either; many of today's tried-and-true brands were founded by older entrepreneurs:

- *Coca-Cola*: After an injury during the Civil War made John Pemberton a morphine addict, he tried developing a morphine substitute using the coca plant (the source of cocaine). New laws forced him to reformulate and in 1886, at the age of 54, Pemberton premiered Coca-Cola.
- *KFC*: Harland Sanders perfected the famous "Secret Recipe" of this fast-food chain (then known as Kentucky Fried Chicken) when he was 52.
- *McDonald's*: Ray Kroc was 52 when he recognized the potential in the McDonald brothers' burgeoning chain of fast-food restaurants, became their partner, and helped create the franchising portion of the business that made the company into the successful worldwide behemoth it is today.[9]

It's not just in the food industry where late bloomers have made names for themselves. Designers Vera Wang and Carolina Herrera were both in their 40s when they struck out in the fiercely competitive fashion world. When her best-selling book *Mastering the Art of French Cooking* was published, Julia Child was already 49. Morgan Freeman didn't land his first big role (in *Glory*) until he was 52. And it wasn't until she was 75 that the artist known as Grandma Moses picked up a paintbrush. Age just has no relevance to success.

That said, for every Colonel Sanders, there's a Mark Zuckerberg out there just waiting to put his idea in action. Numerous young minds have built their ideas into successful companies or organizations. Take the following examples:

- *LightBot*: Danny Yaroslavski was 23 when *Forbes* profiled him for one of its 2015 "30 Under 30" features because of his company's success in teaching kids as young as four coding skills through games.[10]
- *Are You Kidding*: When he was just five (that's not a typo), Sebastian Martinez started designing socks and raked in $15,000 in his first year.[11]
- *Chalk.com*: After noticing how much administrative work his high school teacher had to deal with, William Zhou was inspired to create a solution. The company launched when Zhou was 20, and by 2015 Chalk.com was being used in more than 20,000 schools.[12]

These examples illustrate that creativity and your company's "next big idea" could come from employees of any age.

Workplace demographics are constantly changing, so it's important for everyone to approach each other with consideration and without age-related biases. Everyone wants to be respected and relevant in the workplace, so leave the "too young" and "too old" assumptions behind and focus on who people really are and what they can actually do.

MANAGING WORKERS OLDER THAN YOU

It's always been a reality that employers bring in new blood to shake things up. Throughout my two decades of managing people, I've always had someone working for me who was older than me. Here are a few tips on how to make this situation work for everyone involved:

- *Seek their input.* As previously discussed, you don't need to know everything. Use their experience as a sounding board. You're still the one who has to make the decision, but there's no reason why you shouldn't get their input. Considering all the angles can only help you make a better decision.
- *Respect their working style.* Millennials typically take a team approach to problem solving by bantering around ideas. That probably won't be the preferred style for your Gen Xer or Boomer subordinates. Respect their right to go off and brainstorm on their own before getting your approval to move forward. Don't assume that your style is the only (or right) approach.
- *Be understanding.* Look, it's tough to work for someone younger than you. Try to see the situation from your employees' perspective and give them time to adjust. That doesn't mean they get to disrespect you, but be okay

about them taking baby steps to adjust to you while you, as their manager, take giant steps to work with them. (It's all right if you're going more than halfway. You're still the boss.)

- *Communicate often and well.* Good leadership at every level requires managers to be good communicators. Rarely can people be great leaders if they can't communicate their vision, set expectations, and then coach and mentor employees to achieve those goals. You have to be able to motivate employees of all ages—and without assuming that because someone has been in the office longer than you that he or she will know what you want. Among the 10,000-plus employees I've managed, I've yet to find anyone with mind-reading capabilities.
- *Create mentoring situations.* Young can learn from old, old can learn from young. Make employees teaching their coworkers skills a natural part of coming to work so no one feels weird when being mentored or mentoring someone from a different generation. Learning never stops, so make sure everyone has an opportunity to teach what he or she knows and to learn new skills. *Everyone* wins.
- *Make decisions, then stand by them.* If you're someone who needs 100 percent of the information before you can move forward, you really need to take a step back and decide if leading is right for you. To be a leader you need to be able to make decisions with the facts you do have and then stand by them (though be prepared to reevaluate if your information changes).
- *Treat all of your employees as individuals—but also treat them equally.* Each of your employees will learn at a different pace, know different things, and have his or her own strengths and weaknesses. Differences are good, and understanding them can help you manage each employee to his or her best. However, don't show favoritism to employees of a certain age (such as those of your own generation). Treat everyone with the same respect in order to garner respect in return.
- *Be the boss, but don't be bossy.* The ancient Chinese philosopher Laozi wrote, "A leader is best when people barely know he exists; when his work is done, his aim fulfilled, they will say: we did it ourselves."

As I've pointed out many times throughout this book, managing employees is hard. It can be even more challenging if the manager is older than his or her employee. But if both parties approach the situation in a respectful manner, it can be far less difficult to handle than they might expect.

THE CONSEQUENCES OF NOT BEING INCLUSIVE

Good intentions and company profits aside, there's also a little thing called the law that prohibits managers from making decisions based on federally protected categories such as age, ethnicity, religion, gender, and disability status. If you're new to managing employees, it's critical that you review your company's antiharassment policies and familiarize yourself with the legal requirements surrounding hiring and promotion decisions and managing in general. Because those laws extend beyond your direct reports to include contractors, customers, or any third-party employees, you should assume that anyone you come in contact with should not be evaluated based on any protected categories. (And if you have any doubts about what those are, see your HR department.)

In the context of managing various generations, not only is it unfair to pass judgment based on age, but doing so can also be illegal, particularly when a decision to hire or fire is involved. (Unfortunately, the Age Discrimination in Employment Act [ADEA] of 1967 protects only workers who are at least 40 years old, so younger generations aren't protected by federal legislation from age-based discrimination.)[13] Even though there are laws against age discrimination, it's often not taken as seriously as racial, sexual, and other forms of discrimination and has therefore become extremely pervasive. Consequently, many people over the age of 50 are afraid that, if they lose their jobs, they won't be able to find new ones, because many companies are unwilling to take a chance on older employees—even though many of them are in the prime of their careers and are brimming with ideas. And even if someone suspects he or she has been a victim of age discrimination, it can be difficult to prove that age was the real reason behind an employment-related decision. So although the ADEA exists, it can be difficult to enforce.

NOTES

1. Roosevelt, Thomas R., Jr. *Beyond Race and Gender: Unleashing the Power of Your Total Work Force by Managing Diversity.* New York: Amacom, 1991.

2. Gladwell, Malcolm. *Blink: The Power of Thinking Without Thinking.* New York: Little, Brown and Co., 2005.

3. Durant, Will. *The Story of Philosophy.* New York: Simon & Schuster, 1926, 76.

4. Meyers, Joyce. *Making Good Habits, Breaking Bad Habits: 14 New Behaviors That Will Energize Your Life.* New York: Faith Words, 2013.

5. Sheff, David. "Interview with Steve Jobs." *Playboy.* February 1985. http://reprints.longform.org/playboy-interview-steve-jobs.

6. Knight, Rebecca. "Managing People from 5 Generations." *Harvard Business Review* online. September 25, 2014. http://hbr.org/2014/09/managing-people-from-5-generations.

7. Tannen, Deborah. *You Just Don't Understand: Men and Women in Conversation.* New York: Morrow, 1990.

8. Schmalbruch, Sarah. "Some of the Most Successful Businesses in the U.S. Were Started by Entrepreneurs over Age 50." *Business Insider* website. November 12, 2014. http://www.businessinsider.com/entrepreneurs-over-50-2014-11.

9. Ibid.

10. Howard, Caroline. "Code and College Readiness Are Reinventing Education on 30 Under 30." *Forbes* online. January 5, 2015. http://www.forbes.com/sites/carolinehoward/2015/01/05/code-and-college-readiness-are-reinventing-education-on-30-under-30/#266004b65bf5.

11. Whitten, Sarah. "8 Young Entrepreneurs Making Serious $$$." CNBC website. July 27, 2015. http://www.cnbc.com/2015/07/27/8-young-entrepreneurs-making-serious.html.

12. Ma, Jason. "Twelve of Today's Most Impressive Young Entrepreneurs." *Forbes* online. February 24, 2015. http://www.forbes.com/sites/jasonma/2015/02/24/twelve-of-todays-most-impressive-young-entrepreneurs/#3c8b6f18102b.

13. The Age Discrimination in Employment Act of 1967. US Equal Opportunity Employment Commission website. http://www.eeoc.gov/laws/statutes/adea.cfm.

PROMOTING GROWTH OPPORTUNITIES

What people know is less important than who they are. Hiring ... is not about finding people with the right experience. It's about finding people with the right mindset.

—Peter Carbonara, "Hire for Attitude, Train for Skill"[1]

I n every management position I've held, I've found that for potential new hires, an aptitude for learning is just as important as the degrees they've earned. Sometimes attitude and aptitude are the *most* important factors, because the technical aspects of certain positions can be taught. By surrounding yourself with smart people who display an eagerness to tackle new challenges, you can prepare your department not only to solve today's problems, but also to tackle tomorrow's challenges (even those that are still completely unknown).

At Oxygen, I was asked to take on risk management following the departure of the controller. I had no experience in this area (which focused on company insurance issues, such as workers' compensation and directors' and officers' insurance) but jumped at the chance to learn more and to expand my skill set. Not everyone is so eager to embrace such opportunities, though, especially when, at first glance, they don't seem to align with an employee's current interests or goals.

For example, while in this position I learned that a Millennial employee in finance had declined an invitation to pick up risk management skills because he thought the field sounded "boring." After speaking with him about his career goals, I was able to help him make the connection between his desire to run his own company someday and the importance of insurance for such an endeavor. Following our discussion, he decided to get more involved in risk management and loved the actuarial stuff so much that he eventually took a job with a boutique insurance firm!

This experience served as a bracing reminder that it's impossible to know how "boring" (or fascinating!) something can be without giving it a try—and that jumping in to lend a hand and try something new can be a tremendous career boost, too. It's important that both you and your employees approach new assignments as opportunities to learn something that can expand your skill set and make you more valuable to your organization (whether that's your current company, a future employer, or a business that you start on your own).

John F. Kennedy wrote, "Leadership and learning are indispensable to each other."[2] Over five decades later, those words still ring true: learning never goes out of style. Being continually open to learning new things and fostering a "can do" attitude can position anyone—whether a workforce veteran or a novice—not only to excel at his or her work but to move up the corporate ladder faster. Keep in mind, though, that there's a big difference between projects that offer growth opportunities and tasks that are time-sucking busywork. If you find yourself faced with busywork, think twice about raising your hand (especially if you're already stretched too thin). The ability to say "yes" and take on new challenges can be a positive attribute, but if it leads to missed deadlines, decreased quality, excessive work hours (which in turn can lead to burnout), or an ever-growing (and never-shrinking) to-do list, it could instead turn into a liability.

In spite of the widespread perception that Millennials need more external motivation and encouragement than other generations, it's not only new or young workers who benefit from reminders to keep learning. Experienced employees (and managers, too!) need to remember to keep their skills fresh by asking for more responsibility, by seeking exposure to teams that are tackling new and exciting opportunities within the company, or by finding ways to innovate on their own! The goal is to be learning continuously, even when in the same job.

THE POWER OF EFFECTIVE DELEGATION

Management conversations don't always mention *delegation* and *training* in the same breath. But anyone who's tried to learn a new skill knows that only so much learning can be accomplished through talking—a reality confirmed by numerous studies in recent years and observed as far back as the third century BCE, when the Chinese philosopher Xun Kuang observed, "Tell me, and I forget. Teach me, and I may remember. Involve me, and I learn."[3] In other words, at some point, it's time to actually *do the work*. And letting your employees do the work requires learning how to delegate effectively.

Properly delegating projects to employees can have an amazing effect on their attitude. Being "in charge" can be a great motivator (and spark tremendous creativity!). And because no one likes to fail, someone who's responsible for a project is likely to drive himself or herself harder to succeed. When managers don't delegate effectively, they aren't empowering their employees—which in turn can strongly influence how motivated those employees are to accomplish their goals.

How do you know whether you're delegating effectively? A hasty departure by the Millennials in your workforce can certainly indicate that something is amiss. And if your Generation X or Boomer employees won't make decisions and instead defer to you on next steps, that may mean that it's time to reconsider how you delegate at work.

Effective delegation can be one of the most difficult skills for managers to learn. On the typical promotion path, an individual contributor does such a great job that he or she is rewarded with a position that includes direct reports. But people who are newly promoted to manager positions don't suddenly have all the knowledge and skills they need to delegate well (even though some may have an aptitude for it). Much of delegation needs to be learned on the job.

The challenge with managing is to be able to let employees tackle projects *as they see fit*. A lot of managers think they are delegating when they're actually just telling their employees the exact steps to follow in order to complete a project. That's not delegating—that's assigning tasks. A project that is truly delegated to another person empowers him or her in these three key areas:

- *Responsibility*: Managers must let employees figure out how to accomplish projects on their own. This doesn't mean telling an employee how to do a project; rather, it means making the employee responsible for determining how to achieve the goal. Should you refrain from providing input or offering suggestions? Of course not. But if you're still dictating the how-tos of a project, then your employee is not fully responsible for it—and you haven't fully delegated it.
- *Authority*: In the delegation process, managers tend to struggle most with ceding authority. As the assigned project progresses, it's important to allow employees to make decisions—and if there aren't any decisions for them to make, then you've probably assigned tasks and not actually delegated. When coaching new managers, ask them to keep in mind the project's ultimate goal and consider how to achieve it. If multiple routes lead to the same outcome, allow your employee to choose his or her own path, because that decision-making process is where he or she will actually learn.
- *Accountability*: When you've assigned projects (or even tasks) to your direct reports, you must hold them accountable for getting them done on time, within budget, and to the quality standards you've established. If problems arise, that doesn't mean you should jump in and resolve them yourself; instead, you should provide feedback and coaching to help the employee get back on track. Sometimes, when a project just isn't going well, you may have to take it back from an employee (I have had to do this myself), because as the manager *you* are the one who's ultimately accountable for it. If you have to resort to that course of action, thoroughly evaluate how you prepared the employee to take on the assignment. What could you have done better? How could you have coached him or her to succeed (without getting too involved yourself)? If an employee repeatedly fails to meet expectations, then perhaps the bulk of the problem lies with him or her. But first ask yourself how you contributed to his or her inability to get the job done.

Empowering employees in these three areas can be challenging to anyone who's new to delegation—and especially to anyone who's new to the workforce. Being in charge for the first time can be scary, so expect more questions from younger employees who are being put in that position for the first time. That said, older workers, too, may be hesitant to make decisions. Because of some bad experiences in the past, they may be afraid of getting their hands slapped (or worse!) if they make mistakes. If you're a new boss and everyone is still trying to figure out your management style, you may find your staff reluctant (or unable) to assume full responsibility, authority, and accountability for projects you delegate to them. Any time you delegate, one of your goals should be to push your employees outside their comfort zones and encourage them to come up with next steps and solutions on their own.

When teaching employees of all ages how to accept delegation, don't just tell them what to do next; instead, have everyone brainstorm solutions together. Filling a whiteboard with potential solutions can really get the creative juices flowing, inspiring everyone to come up with new and terrific ideas. Brainstorming like this with employees a few times helps them learn how to brainstorm on their own so that they need your help only for narrowing down which possibility to pursue. (At that point, once they've already done the heavy lifting, you can brainstorm with them about the pros and cons of the top three options.) By helping employees practice and strengthen the responsibility, authority, and accountability they need to successfully complete delegated projects, this process teaches them how to make decisions and continue to move forward on their own. Eventually, as employees work on these skills, you'll notice that they have fewer questions for you and can complete projects with greater speed and independence.

At this point it's important to clarify that delegation is *not* the same as dumping a project onto an employee (whether a novice learning new skills or a seasoned veteran) and never checking in with him or her about it again. Nor is delegation the same as abdicating responsibility for a project. Because your employees' performance always reflects on you and your ability to engage and motivate, *you* will always be the one who's ultimately accountable for their actions. Therefore, you need to stay involved in every project you delegate (to the point where it's clear that you still care—but not so much that you're micromanaging).

If you're saying to yourself, "Delegation seems like a lot of work," you're right. But there are many good reasons to delegate, including this one (which is perhaps at the top of the list): it frees you up to think strategically and focus on the bigger issues of running a department.

How easily do you get lost in the day-to-day details? If you're overwhelmed with projects or tasks because you're not effectively delegating to your staff, it can be extremely difficult to step back and see the big picture. When you focus too much on your department's tactical concerns and not enough on its strategic role in helping the company achieve its financial goals, you can end up hurting not only your company and your department but your own career, too. So make sure that effective delegation is at the top of your to-do (well) list.

Developing employees through effective delegation allows them to take on more responsibility and thus makes them more valuable to the company. Delegation can engage and motivate employees by giving them opportunities to learn new skills and grow personally. It also helps build a succession plan: when you to move on to other things, your employees move up behind you—and your department's throughput continues without interruption.

Effective delegation requires managers to learn to let go—to step back and let employees do their jobs without too much intervention. Work through this list of questions to make sure that you're delegating properly and giving your employees the information and tools they need to complete their assignments well.

- *Which* one *project or task can you delegate in the next week?* This cannot be a menial assignment; choose something of importance.
- *To whom on your staff will you delegate the project? What do you want them to learn from this experience?* Discussing with your employees what they will gain from being in charge of a project will help engage and motivate them, particularly if they run into problems while working on the assignment.
- *What outcome do you desire, and when does it need to be completed?* Be specific when defining your parameters and convey this information clearly so your employees understand exactly what you expect.
- *What information do your employees need to know in order to* start *on this project?* Don't tell your employees how to do the project; instead, let them suggest how they plan to tackle it.
- *What decisions can your employees make without consulting with you?* Push yourself not to micromanage here. Give your employees the responsibility and authority to accomplish this project on their own.
- *When (and in what form) do you want updates?* If the update mentions problems, ask your employees to come up with solutions. Coach them to come up with possible options (rather than just ask you how to proceed).
- *What happens if your employees fall behind?* Don't automatically take over the project to get it back on track. Instead, focus your efforts on coaching your employees so that *they* can get things back on track (then do more frequent check-ins on the project's progress).

EMPOWER YOUR EMPLOYEES

Empowering employees is certainly an oft-discussed topic, but what exactly does it mean? To empower means "to give official authority or legal power to" do something.[4] That sounds a lot like effective delegation—and, to an extent, it is. To managers, however, the terms have slightly different meanings: empowerment is a tool for motivating employees, whereas delegation is the process of assigning projects and tasks to employees. In short, to be an effective delegator a manager must empower his or her employees. Unfortunately, managers often make the mistake of delegating without empowering. Under those conditions, the employee's learning stops, and the manager still ends up running the project (because he or she has to make every decision). Managers need to be able to let others make decisions and to understand that empowering others is necessary for the department to succeed and, in turn, for the company to succeed. Stephen Covey points out that "an empowered organization is one in which individuals have the knowledge, skill, desire, and opportunity to personally succeed in a way that leads to collective organizational success."[5] And because an organization is only as strong as its weakest link, make sure that your department is leading the pack—and not dragging it down.

If you want to empower your employees effectively, take these actions:

- Encourage employees to achieve outstanding results and push themselves beyond their comfort zones. How can you get them to look past their current skill sets and discover their own untapped potential? How can you prod them to explore beyond their current ways of thinking?
- Motivate employees to accept new challenges with enthusiasm and to push themselves to think outside the box (and not just stick to a "business as usual" mind-set). What new ideas can they bring to the table? How can they make the process better?
- Generate enthusiasm among employees for achieving their goals. How can you use recognition and rewards to encourage employees to continue to grow and learn? How can you get them excited about trying something new (even if it may seem boring at first glance)?

And if you *don't* want to empower your employees, take these actions:

- Give orders and demand action.
- Provide unambiguous, very clear instructions that tell employees *exactly* what to do.
- Give the impression that your employees are not smart enough to figure out solutions without your help ("I know how to do this—and you don't").
- Solve problems for your employees instead of coaching them on how to solve those problems themselves.

In a nutshell, the best way to empower your employees is to clearly articulate to them the goals and your expectations—then get out of their way and let them solve the problem. And avoid making decisions based on age, such as empowering older workers more because you assume their age means they have more experience or withholding such opportunities from younger workers because you assume they aren't yet ready for such responsibility. As you evaluate and refine your empowerment skills, make sure you're treating *all* employees consistently across the board.

ACCOMMODATING DIFFERENT LEARNING STYLES

Each generation has its own learning styles, often shaped to a large degree by the technological innovations during that generation's formative years. Baby Boomers, for example, were tremendously influenced by the development of personal computers, whereas the members of Generation X came of age during the rise of the Internet, and Millennials have grown up surrounded by social media and apps for just about everything. When assigning new or additional responsibilities to an employee, it's critical to understand the learning styles of his or her generation if you want that individual to succeed. In particular, pay attention to the learning options that were available while that person received business training during the early years of his or her career.

Many Baby Boomers received little or no formal business training: for this generation, the prevailing philosophy was often "sink or swim." When training was available, it typically took place in classrooms where the teachers lectured and did 90 percent of the talking (and notes were handwritten with pen or pencil on paper). Baby Boomers may be accustomed to minimal interaction with instructors who stand up and deliver content, but don't assume that the Boomers actively like this style of training: when they were growing up, it was usually the only choice they had. With unions at the top in both power and popularity, apprenticeships (particularly in skilled trades) were one widely used training option. These very structured programs awarded rank and seniority based on how long people had been in their positions and not necessarily on how quickly they picked up their skills. So even if a worker had the knowledge and skill to advance, he (unions were almost entirely male, particularly in the early days) was required to wait until he had a certain number of years under his belt before getting new opportunities, promotions, or other recognition.

The members of Generation X, on the other hand, were much more vocal during their training. They had little tolerance for teachers who droned on; rather than listen silently to lectures, they would instead interrupt with their questions (and then express their displeasure to HR afterward about how boring the class was). Generation X came of age during the early days of online training classes (which, in terms of effectiveness, were definitely a mixed bag). This generation was also the first to use Capstone business simulations, which were first developed in the mid-1980s and quickly skyrocketed in popularity (particularly in business schools).

Last but not least, the Millennials came of age during an era of incredibly rapid technological innovation. Much more than their parents and grandparents, they had more influence over how they were taught as teaching methods changed to accommodate a more team-centric approach. Millennials barely knew a world without the Internet, and they were the first generation to have Wi-Fi in their classrooms and the first generation for which note taking took place mostly on laptops or mobile devices (such as iPads) and not on paper.

Does all of this mean that the best way to communicate with Baby Boomer employees is to lecture at them for an hour? And that the only way to teach Millennials anything is to make them work in teams? Definitely not. But it does mean that managers need to employ a mix of training options in order to reach employees of all generations. For example, when training is done via in-person presentation or lectures, the teacher should make the content available electronically as well (by posting the presentation slides on the company's intranet, perhaps). When training is done online, it should be followed by an in-person Q&A session so employees can revisit the material with the instructor. And every training (whether in person or online) should be accompanied by a review session a few weeks later to see if the employees have come up with any questions since they first learned the material. Combining different media, technologies, and approaches helps ensure that all types of learners understand the training.

Although learning styles can vary from generation to generation, it's critical for managers to keep in mind that learning styles can also vary for reasons that aren't necessarily age related. For example, someone who's more of a visual learner (or hard of hearing) may prefer to have written outlines of the instructor's content; another person might not need or want as much written information. Many engineers (such as me) are very comfortable with agendas and manuals, whereas people with creative tendencies may glean knowledge more readily from discussions, conceptualization exercises, or drawing.

There are many options for conveying information in business training—and technology and new approaches to education keep increasing the possibilities. Here are a few effective strategies for driving home key concepts:

- Show videos or do live in-person demonstrations or role play.
- Create exercises designed to solidify challenging concepts by highlighting and demonstrating their importance (and not merely saying "This is important").
- Ask a lot of questions in class and provide detailed answer sheets that attendees can keep as reference materials.
- Give copies of training materials to attendees so they can take notes in them during the discussions.
- Assign homework (such as books or articles to read).
- Teach via online gaming and training platforms.
- Combine demonstrations with live Q&A periods.
- Offer one-on-one Q&A sessions (which can be particularly beneficial for people who are too shy or otherwise reluctant to ask questions in group settings).
- Conduct one-on-one follow-up sessions with employees at their desks (where, in their own environments, they may be more relaxed and therefore more apt to ask questions).

Sometimes it can be challenging to figure out which techniques to use with which people. But if you're training people who work for you, just *ask* them how they best learn new concepts. If they don't know, keep asking yourself, "Which training methods help them understand and use the new knowledge quicker?" and try different strategies until you find the ones that seem to work best with your employees.

EXPERIENTIAL TRAINING

As stated earlier, when it comes to learning a new skill *doing* is better than *listening*. After more than two decades of "doing" management, I'm certainly much better at it now than I was when I first started. Knowing how effective hands-on training can be, I have tried to provide it for my employees as much as possible over the years.

For example, at Oxygen I arranged to be job-shadowed for a week by junior employees who didn't report directly to me in order to give them perspective on the knowledge their bosses had and on the skills they themselves would need for continued advancement. I arranged for my own direct reports to spend a week job-shadowing other senior executives throughout the company, so they could learn firsthand about challenges that employees were facing and then bring that knowledge back to their own departments. In addition to these job-shadowing opportunities, I also set up monthly lunches at which senior leaders from different departments talked about their jobs. In addition to the stuff they loved (and were clearly most excited about), they also discussed the tasks they least enjoyed and how they pushed themselves to get those done. These sessions were great learning opportunities for everyone: those new to the workforce learned that every job has some inherently boring aspects, and more seasoned workers were reminded to stop procrastinating and get things done.

These activities could work (with modifications, if needed) for nearly any department and provide valuable opportunities for employees to learn through hands-on experience and direct observation. These aren't the only options out there, though. Here are a few other experiential learning practices that can be effective.

- Expose employees to organizations with relationships to the company (e.g., visit a vendor, take a trip to customer's site).
- Allow employees to do a temporary rotation in areas in which they need to improve their skills or to which they need to gain exposure for continued growth.
- Invite employees to spearhead projects in areas in which they need improvement.
- Ask employees to read case studies and books on issues that are relevant to your organization, then present their ideas to and lead discussion with fellow executives. (Consider asking the CEO for book recommendations!)
- Encourage employees to develop leadership and management skills by volunteering for local industry organizations, nonprofit groups, school organizations, or community-based programs.

When considering training opportunities for your employees, keep in mind one critical goal: *all* employees need to understand how your company makes money, how individual department budgets connect to the organization's products and services, and how all that information describes the company's financial health.

Unfortunately, most employees (including some senior leaders) are woefully ignorant in these areas. Don't let yours be among them: have your HR and finance departments team up to teach classes on budgeting and its connection to your company's financial well-being, and then assign budget-line items to your direct reports and have them track and report on those items each month. Even when these items are typically smallish dollar amounts, studying them teaches your employees what is expected during the monthly review with the controller or the CFO. That's knowledge of value to every employee, regardless of position or status. By starting small, you can help your employees develop the expertise and confidence to manage ever-increasing amounts of money so they are prepared for the day they're promoted into a position that requires them to manage their own general ledger-line items. And an added bonus to teaching your entire staff fiscal responsibility is that they'll soon be identifying cost-cutting measures, because they'll be as eager as your CFO to save money and improve the company's finances.

ESTABLISH A MENTORING PROGRAM

One of the best experiential learning opportunities a company can provide is a mentoring program. Recognizing the multitude of benefits that such programs convey to both protégé and mentor, most Fortune 500 companies (currently about 70 percent of them) offer them to their employees.[6] Mentoring employees (especially new hires) can lead to better retention, and mentoring aspiring talent can form the cornerstone of succession planning. Mentoring programs traditionally pair a junior employee with a more experienced colleague, but there's no need to stick only to this format. Reverse mentoring, for example, can help senior executives keep up with cutting-edge technology and with company issues that are usually only on the radar of junior staff. Group or situational mentoring is also on the rise to address issues such as diversity or to provide high-potential training. If your company doesn't have a formal mentoring program, create your own in whatever form best meets your needs! As you do so, establish mentoring relationships for your employees by tapping fellow executives (and agreeing to mentor their employees in return).

NOTES

1. Carbonara, Peter. "Hire for Attitude, Train for Skill." *Fast Company* online. August 31, 1996. http://www.fastcompany.com/26996/hire-attitude-train-skill. Used with permission of FastCompany.com. Copyright 2016. All rights reserved.
2. Kennedy, John F. "Undelivered Remarks for Dallas Citizens Council, Trade Mart, Dallas, Texas, 22 November 1963." John F. Kennedy Presidential Library and Museum archives. 1963. http://www.jfklibrary.org/Asset-Viewer/Archives/JFKPOF-048-022.aspx.

3. Knoblock, John. *Xunzi: A Translation and Study of the Complete Works, Books 7–16*. Palo Alto, CA: Stanford University Press, 1990.

4. *Merriam-Webster's Collegiate Dictionary*, 11th ed. *s.v.* "Empower."

5. Covey, Stephen R. *Principle-Centered Leadership*. New York: Simon & Schuster, 1992.

6. Gutner, Toddi. "Finding Anchors in the Storm: Mentors." *Wall Street Journal* online. January 27, 2009. http://www.wsj.com/articles/SB123301451869117 603.

Chapter 7

MANAGING DIFFERENCES IN WORK ETHIC

The first and paramount responsibility of anyone who purports to manage is to manage self; one's own integrity, character, ethics, knowledge, wisdom, temperament, words, and acts ...

—Dee Hock[1]

O f all the areas of conflict among the generations, work ethic is certainly the most challenging to overcome, partly because it's an elusive trait to begin with. An Internet search for a definition, for example, will yield many variations with subtle, yet quite meaningful, differences:

- "a belief in the moral benefit and importance of work and its inherent ability to strengthen character"[2]
- "a belief in work as a moral good"[3]
- "the principle that hard work is intrinsically virtuous or worthy of reward"[4]

These definitions highlight one major area of difference among the generations: the degree to which work and the corporate entity are regarded as "good." Such ideals have waned in recent decades, and many Millennials don't subscribe to the notion that workers should put work ethic above all else. Interestingly, although both Baby Boomers and Generation Xers grew up amid major corporate downsizing, both generations still value a strong work ethic and believe that employees have a moral obligation to work hard for their companies. To illustrate the different generations' ideas about work ethic in today's corporate America, consider this hypothetical scenario:

Bob works at Company XYZ, and his daughter's big soccer game kicks off at 4 p.m. on a Tuesday. Does he leave the office early so he can make it to the game?

☐ If Bob is a Baby Boomer, he is more likely to stick to his work regimen (and might even have workaholic tendencies). This generation views hard work as sacred, so he probably wouldn't think twice about missing the game in favor of staying in the office. He also wouldn't feel guilty about this choice.

☐ If Bob is a Generation Xer, he likely favors work-life balance and would therefore rearrange his work schedule so he could attend the soccer match. At the game, he'd keep checking his e-mail so he could stay up to date on work happenings. If he were unable to move a critical meeting, he'd probably skip the game in favor of his work priorities (and probably feel guilty about doing so).

☐ If Bob is a Millennial, he probably doesn't equate his physical presence at work with getting the job done—so it would never occur to him to miss the game in favor of staying in the office. The members of this generation have grown up with technology and are adept at using it to get plenty of work done outside of traditional office spaces.

On this subject, Gen Xers straddle the line between the Boomers and Millennials. Even as they strive to achieve work-life balance, Gen Xers still lean toward spending time in the office if that is what's needed to get the job done—a mindset they learned from their Baby Boomer parents, mentors, and bosses.

Another work-ethic-related notion on which the generations hold different ideas is face time, the practice of being in the office and doing work at one's desk during regular business hours (usually 9 a.m. to 5 p.m.). Millennials, who prioritize flexibility in their work arrangements, aren't big fans of face time. Baby Boomers and Gen Xers, on the other hand, were raised on the practice. If you want to change face time policies at your company and you're a younger manager dealing with older employees, keep in mind that you're trying to alter years (or even decades) of behavior, so don't expect change to happen overnight. Similarly, if you're an older manager dealing with younger employees, make it a priority to keep up with changing workplace norms and learn how to manage workers who aren't sitting right outside your office. You and your employees *can* adapt to new things—you just have to step up your managing game and figure out what works for both you and your direct reports.

Before I tackle a full discussion of work ethic, I want to make one very important point: even though many members of older generations grumble to the contrary, Millennials *do* work hard. Unlike older generations, who usually work without question on the tasks to which they are assigned, Millennials will actually ask *why* something needs to be done (a tendency that can drive some old-school managers crazy!). Millennials need to be inspired by what they do before they commit a task, but when they do commit they are fully on board. Their high rates of educational achievement (they've done more college and graduate study than any previous generation) highlight how the power of *why* can motivate them (they recognize the long-term financial benefits, in terms of future income, of postsecondary education) and demonstrate their commitment to complete tasks that have meaning for them.

DEFINING WORK ETHIC

As a manager, you need to discuss your expectations with your employees (as addressed in chapter 4). Your expectations are shaped by your understanding and definition of work ethic, so make sure to communicate that, too, to your employees, because it will influence their work. With that in mind, to help you define work ethic to your employees, identify which of these personal attributes resonate with your management style:

- *Honest.* Be truthful in your dealings with employees, vendors, customers, and anyone else with whom you come in contact on behalf of the company. Do not intentionally mislead or misrepresent the company in its business dealings with others. (Honesty is the cornerstone of *any* definition of work ethic.)
- *Full of integrity.* Maintain high-quality standards despite schedule pressures. Follow your own standards and exceed what is required. Demonstrate and uphold values and principles that create a climate of trust.
- *Law-abiding.* Act within the statutes of the law and the company's rules and regulations. Don't look for ways to cut corners and beat the system.
- *Trustworthy.* Speak the truth even when no one else does. Be candid and forthcoming. Give credit freely for others' accomplishments. Stand by your commitments and own up to your mistakes. Don't betray confidences (unless maintaining them supports an unethical act). Keep your promises. Be on time and prepared for meetings.
- *Fair.* Be fair and just in dealings with employees. Value and support diversity and inclusion across the board. When you are wrong, admit it and be willing to change your opinion.
- *Respectful of others.* Display grace under pressure and don't lash out at employees, even when deadlines are tight or tempers flare. Show respect for all your colleagues (whether they report to you or not) by seeking their input when trying to solve problems.
- *Dedicated.* Deliver outstanding results (not just "good enough") results in all that you do. Don't stop until the job is done and done right.
- *Determined.* Continually strive to solve problems, even in the face of adversity. Resolve to seek better and more innovative ways of doing things. Don't accept business as usual.
- *Accountable.* Take personal responsibility for your actions and outcomes. When things don't go as planned, admit your mistakes and avoid making excuses (or blaming others).
- *Concern for others.* Show gratitude to direct reports and colleagues who work hard. Say thank you when your employees complete tasks and projects.
- *Encouraging.* Help your employees achieve their professional goals (even if that leads them out of your department). Care about their success.

I've intentionally omitted loyalty from this discussion of work ethic, because the meaning of loyalty has shifted greatly over the past few decades. As I mentioned in chapter 2, Millennials watched their parents live through the decline of corporate loyalty and saw them begin to job-hop as better opportunities presented themselves. In the wake of those experiences and in the context of today's job market, Millennials have taken job-hopping one (or several) steps further: their loyalty to companies tends to last only about two or three years, tops. Before you judge the Millennials harshly for this, though, remember, that companies and especially managers need to *earn* loyalty—and in many cases they don't. Connected to the lack of loyalty is a decrease in automatically bestowing respect for someone with a title. After hearing their Generation X parents openly discuss their own lack of trust in corporate leaders. Millennials are unlikely to give their trust and respect to any manager who hasn't earned it from them. Gen Zers are expected to continue this trend.

THE IMPORTANCE OF MISSION TO MILLENNIALS

Although Boomer or Generation Xers often started working while they were still in school (I baled hay and mowed lawns during high school, for example), Millennials often have no work experience before joining corporate America after college graduation. They tend to spend a lot of time in extracurricular activities (where participation is encouraged by their parents as a way to increase their college admission chances), and because their parents have more disposable income than previous generations, Millennials don't necessarily need to work for spending money. And the Generation Z employees who are poised to enter the workforce lack work experience for similar reasons.[5]

What does that mean for your company? Because work ethic is mostly learned on the job, new hires who lack actual work experience may not yet have a fully formed sense of what this means (beyond fragments they learn from their parents). They'll develop their own as they work for you. They'll also be influenced by what they learn from other bosses, their mentors, and their colleagues—and by their own personal values. Beyond a strong desire for work-life balance, for many Millennials, values and work ethic will often align with a greater mission or purpose.

According to a survey by the nonprofit group Net Impact, 59 percent of Millennials in the workforce have the "desire for a job that can make a difference."[6] Other studies shed light on additional interests that can be relevant to the hiring and retention of Millennials:

- Roughly 80 percent of Millennials want to work for companies that care about their impact on society and the world.[7]
- Because of their high concern about the environment (documented in a recent Pew survey)[8] many Millennials are choosing to get around by bike or public transportation instead of by car (and are waiting longer to get their driver's licenses).[9]

Senior leaders need to pay attention to these trends and should expect the concepts of sustainability and corporate responsibility to increasingly shape Millennials' ideas about their own work ethic and their expectations of corporate behavior. Millennials place a high value on seeing companies institute sustainable sourcing and production practices. According to a recent Nielsen global online study, Millennials have demonstrated a willingness to pay more for "sustainable offerings" that help the planet, and Generation Z is exhibiting similar tendencies: the rise in the percentage of respondents aged 15 to 20 who are willing to pay more for products and services that come from companies who are committed to positive social and environmental impact was up from 55 percent in 2014 to 72 percent in 2015.[10] According to Grace Farraj, senior vice president of public development and sustainability at Nielsen, "Brands that establish a reputation for environmental stewardship among today's youngest consumers have an opportunity to not only grow market share but build loyalty among the power-spending Millennials of tomorrow, too."[11]

A Hewitt and Associates study found that employees at companies that prioritize sustainability and social responsibility tend to be more engaged and committed.[12] According to the Society for Human Resources Management, employees who work at companies with strong sustainability programs exhibit many more positive attributes than employees working at companies with poor sustainability programs: morale was 55 percent better, business processes were 43 percent more efficient, public image was 43 percent stronger, and employee loyalty was 38 percent better.[13] Now is the time for your company to make sustainability and corporate responsibility priorities in order to attract and retain employees.

CONNECTING COMPANY MISSION TO SOCIAL GOALS

Tying social goals to the company mission is another way to demonstrate (and reward) ideal employee behavior. For example, consider Starbucks, whose website states a commitment to having a positive impact on the communities the company serves by:

- Sourcing ethically and sustainably
- Creating opportunities through education, training, and employment
- Leading in green retail by minimizing its environmental footprint
- Encouraging service and civic engagement[14]

Similarly, the mission statement of the grocery chain Whole Foods includes eight core values that marry the company's ethics (support for local and global communities, for example, and the practice and advancement of environmental stewardship) with its mission to "create wealth through profits and growth."[15] Smart companies infuse their mission statements with social values that will attract and engage employees. Smart managers then ensure that each and every one of their employees understands the ethical elements of the company's mission, thus helping to secure greater engagement—and perhaps more loyalty—from those employees.

If your company doesn't have a mission statement that ties in directly to corporate responsibility, you can still use the mission statement you do have. As I discussed in chapter 4, tying individual goals to company goals can help motivate and engage employees of all ages, because it makes an employee feels that he or she is part of the bigger picture of the organization and not just a mere cog in the corporate wheel. Savvy managers spend time explaining to employees the company's mission, vision, and goals, and then make the connection between each employee's tasks and projects and the achievement of those goals. It's especially important for managers to do this with the Millennial set, because if you want their work ethic to include getting the job done on time per the quality standards you've laid out, they need to understand why it matters—what makes this assignment important in the grand scheme of things. If they (or you) cannot make that connection, don't be surprised if your Millennial employees challenge the need to do that task, do subpar work on it, or even leave the company altogether.

Remember, if you're a Baby Boomer or a Gen Xer who's managing Millennials, mission matters—particularly when you're looking to align your work ethic with that of your employees. If you're a Millennial manager supervising Boomers, chances are they may need less tie-in to the company mission because they are more prone to "get it done" instead of asking why a task needs to be accomplished. Gen Xers are somewhere in the middle: they sometimes ask questions, but usually don't offer as much resistance as the Millennials. Regardless of the ages of your employees, though, it's always a good idea to discuss with all of them how their work connects to the company's greater mission.

One final reminder on Millennials: if you can't connect their individual goals to the larger company operation or if their assignments run counter to their sense of purpose, you'll have a much harder time keeping them around.[16] Unlike earlier generations, many Millennials have the option to move back in with Mom and Dad if they don't like a job or don't believe in its mission (or don't know what it is because their manager didn't make the connection for them). Without the pressure to pay rent, they don't need to put up with a company or a job that doesn't engage and motivate them.

WHAT MANAGERS CAN DO

Baby Boomers believe they need to pay their dues and work hard before receiving a promotion. Generation Xers operate from a "what's in it for me?" perspective and will jump from company to company in pursuit of better opportunities. And Millennials prioritize their own individualism. With different generations holding such varying ideas about work ethic and what defines professional behavior, it's no wonder that work ethic is such challenging territory for managers to address. Handling differences in work ethic is a key part of effectively managing employees in a multigenerational workplace.

As a manager, you should know what you need to do to retain employees of all ages. First, understand each generation's motivations for being in the workplace:

- Boomers are the most loyal of the generations—they want to trust their employers and in return for that trust, they won't job-hop as much as either

Gen Xers or Millennials. They value being respected for their knowledge and experience and like to teach others. They are comfortable working alone and don't require a lot of feedback.

- Gen Xers prefer to work alone, and they place a high value on their individual freedom (including setting their own hours and incorporating work-from-home options). They thrive on being offered a variety of challenges and being given responsibility and creative input. If they don't receive such opportunities, they'll move.
- Millennials need more detailed instructions on what is expected, including why their work is important (and how it fits into the overall company plan). Don't micromanage—let them figure out how to get the job done. As a manager, if you engage them from Day 1, they will work hard and show loyalty. If you lose them out of the gate, they'll leave (even if they don't have another job lined up).

These are some broad observations to get you started. But because no two people have identical interests or motivations (even if they're of the same generation), it's *critical* to have a conversation with each of your employees in order to understand how he or she best likes to be managed. Questions to discuss include:

- How much feedback do you need or want on individual projects? How much feedback is too much?
- How do you want to receive feedback (e.g., by e-mail, by text, in person)?
- How often (e.g., weekly, biweekly, monthly) do you expect to discuss your performance, including career development discussions?
- What is your expectation of my availability when you have questions?
- What's the best way to communicate with you on a daily or weekly basis?
- How do you plan to keep me up to speed on your projects?
- What if there's an emergency and I need information quickly—what is the best way to reach you if you're not at your desk?
- As your manager, how can I help you feel as though you're a part of the department and the organization?
- What will kill your enthusiasm for the department and the company?
- What can I do to make you feel comfortable about coming to speak with me if you feel yourself start to disengage from the company?

After discussing these questions with your direct report, think of the treasure trove of information you'll have to help you manage him or her effectively! Throughout my career as a manager, I would ask a new hire these questions when her or she started and then again at three months; I would also discuss them about every six months with all of my employees, regardless of how long they had been with me. My employees' expectations of me changed—and their need for my input and guidance decreased—as they grew more confident in their abilities and comfortable in the organization.

Your input on these questions is just as important, by the way! For example, if you're a Millennial managing a team of Boomers and Gen Xers, you'll probably want more frequent check-ins while the project is under way. Your team may take this to mean you don't trust them to get the job accomplished and may consider this micromanaging. So be sure to explain what information you need and why and how it's designed to keep you in the loop and up to speed (and not to help you second-guess them). Agree on when and how often you'll receive updates and at which decision points you need to be brought in. Regardless of your age or your employees' age, make sure your behavior doesn't cross over to micromanaging, because then your employees will basically stop working and wait for you to give them explicit directions (something that defeats your delegation tactics and requires double work on your part!).

During a new hire's first week (and then as needed going forward), I also have a one-on-one discussion with each employee about his or her work-life balance expectations. Throughout my management career, I typically expected new employees to prioritize work as much as possible in the beginning, because I wanted them to be readily available for in-person check-ins and feedback. As soon as an employee found his or her grove, though, I made it clear that I was flexible on his or her needs outside the office, including working from home, as long as we reached an agreement on how the employee would keep me up to speed on progress on projects.

Having these discussions up front and as often as needed takes the pressure off, because they enable you to find out what your employees need without having to guess. Calibrating expectations on both ends of this relationship helps your employee be the best he or she can be—and helps you be a great manager.

WHAT COMPANIES CAN DO

At a minimum, companies need to define what they mean by *work ethic* in terms of professional conduct in the office. Laying out in crystal-clear terms what constitutes ethical behavior and then communicating those guidelines to employees is *critical*. After all, if employees don't know how the company defines work ethic, how can they be held accountable to company standards? So provide a definition of work ethic as well as pertinent examples that illustrate it. At the same time, be sure to acknowledge the different generations' ideas about work ethic (particularly regarding loyalty, work-life balance, and face time). Highlighting some of those differences—and then discussing them together—can help everyone find more common ground. Here are some examples of such differences:

- Loyalty for a Boomer is a minimum 10-year commitment, whereas a Millennial thinks staying 3 years at a job shows loyalty.

- Boomers work hard while they're in the office and then leave action items behind when they walk out at 5:00 p.m.
- Instead of balancing work and life priorities, Gen Xers and Millennials blend their work and home lives by constantly checking e-mail outside the office.
- Older generations value face time, whereas younger generations think in terms of *how* the job gets done, not *where* it gets done.

Having led such discussions among my direct reports, I've always found it to be an eye-opening conversation for employees of all ages and experience levels (myself included).

NOTES

1. Hock, Dee. *Birth of the Chaordic Age.* Oakland, Calif.: Berrett-Koehler Publishers, 2000. Reprinted with permission of the publisher. All rights reserved.
2. Dictionary.com. *s.v.* "Work ethic."
3. Merriam-Webster.com. *s.v.* "Work ethic."
4. OxfordDictionaries.com. *s.v.* "Work ethic."
5. The Council of Economic Advisers. "15 Economic Facts About Millennials." The White House website. October 2014. http://www.whitehouse.gov/sites/default/files/docs/millennials_report.pdf.
6. Zukin, Cliff, and Mark Szeltner. "Talent Report: What Workers Want in 2012." Net Impact website. 2012. http://netimpact.org/sites/default/files/documents/what-workers-want-2012.pdf.
7. Yuen, Justin, and Richard Rosen. "Why Be a B Corp? Ask a Millennial." Sustainable Brands website. July 25, 2013. http://www.sustainablebrands.com/news_and_views/communications/why-be-b-corp-ask-millennial.
8. Pew Research Center. "The Generation Gap and the 2012 Election." Pew Research Center website. November 3, 2011. http://www.people-press.org/files/legacy-pdf/11-3-11%20Generations%20Release.pdf.
9. NPR. "Millennials Choosing Buses and Bikes over Buicks." NPR website. May 17, 2013. http://www.npr.org/templates/story/story.php?storyId=184775458.
10. Nielsen. "The Sustainability Imperative: New Insights on Consumer Expectations." Nielsen website. October 2015. http://www.nielsen.com/content/dam/corporate/us/en/reports-downloads/2015-reports/global-sustainability-report-oct-2015.pdf.
11. Ibid.
12. Hewitt Associates. "Employees Identify 'The Green 30' Organizations Based on Eco-Friendly Programs and Practices." Hewitt Associates website.

April 22, 2010. http://ceplb03.hewitt.com/bestemployers/canada/pdfs/Hewitt TheGreen30_eng.pdf.

13. Society for Human Resources Management, BSR, and Aurosoorya. "Advancing Sustainability: HR's Role," Society for Human Resources Management website. 2011. https://www.shrm.org/Research/SurveyFindings/Articles/Documents/11-0066_AdvSustainHR_FNL_FULL.pdf.

14. Starbucks. "What Is the Role and Responsibility of a For-Profit, Public Company?" Starbucks website. http://www.starbucks.com/responsibility.

15. Whole Foods. "Our Core Values." Whole Foods website. http://www.wholefoodsmarket.com/mission-values/core-values.

16. Bureau of Labor Statistics. "Employee Tenure Summary." Bureau of Labor Statistics website. September 18, 2014. http://www.bls.gov/news.release/tenure.nr0.htm.

Chapter 8

MANAGING DIFFERENT WORK-LIFE BALANCE EXPECTATIONS

I risk my life for my own work, and my reason has half foundered in it.
—Vincent van Gogh[1]

Each generation introduces a new set of values into the workplace, and although work-life balance has been on the radar for previous generations, it's certainly of more importance to Millennials, with 48 percent of them choosing workplace flexibility over pay.[2] This preference comes as no surprise, because Millennials witnessed firsthand both the long hours their parents had to put in to get ahead in corporate America and companies' ruthless downsizing for purely financial gain (usually in pursuit of greater shareholder profits). Many Millennials "are largely unconvinced that what they would have to give up [in their personal lives] is worth such a sacrifice."[3] In addition, with the rise in technology that lets employees work from anywhere, spending 9 or 10 hours in the office looks less and less appealing to Millennials (and even more so to the Gen Zers after them). This doesn't mean that Millennials aren't interested in getting ahead (on the contrary, most are gunning to get promoted as quickly as possible), but it does mean that they have different priorities from their predecessors.

Although the Millennials' emphasis on work-life balance has had a positive effect for *all* generations (both Baby Boomers and Gen Xers are also demanding—and receiving—more flexibility), it's still a source of conflict between older managers and their younger employees, because Millennial expectations go far beyond the comfort zone of previous generations. Gen X managers are in a particularly precarious position—their work ethic was heavily influenced by their Boomer and Traditionalist predecessors, but they also have to navigate the new rules of the Millennial generation.

THE BIRTH OF WORK-LIFE BALANCE

There are many definitions for *work-life balance*, although most are similar to this one: "the amount of time you spend doing your job compared with the amount of time you spend with your family and doing things you enjoy."[4] The term first appeared in print in the mid-1980s but it didn't really become popular until the early 2000s (appearing 400-plus times in print a year). In 2005 it showed up 10,000 times, and since then its significance in work-related discussions has only increased.[5] What's behind this trend?

Although younger managers often dismiss Baby Boomers as being "antiquated," it's worth noting that the Boomers invented many of the technologies that have enabled later generations to work outside the office: personal computers, the Internet, the World Wide Web, mobile phones, and PDAs, to name just a few. Gen X started the trend toward a more relaxed work environment, introducing the corporate world to casual Fridays (which eventually led to "casual all the time"), and embraced e-mail, teleconferencing, videoconferencing, telepresence, and other tools that give workers more flexibility in where and how they do their jobs. Although pagers and mobile phones helped employees get out of the office, employees were still tethered to desktop or laptop computers for e-mail until BlackBerry's devices hit the market in 1999. Mobilizing e-mail was a corporate game changer that allowed employees to stay connected while on the go.

With the mantra "Out of the office, but still connected," Gen Xers led the charge to work from home (much to the chagrin of their Boomer managers). Unfortunately, that mantra took on a life of its own, with technology allowing employees to work 24 hours a day and 7 days a week. Another phenomenon also occurred: with employees being able to access e-mail all the time, managers then began expecting replies from them around the clock as well. In the early days of Oxygen Media (around 2000–2001), I told my employees that although I sent e-mail at all hours because my long-time insomnia often kept me awake in the middle of the night, I did not expect them to send replies until they arrived in the office the next morning. In the event of a true emergency, I would actually call someone on the phone rather than send him or her an e-mail. Needless to say, my staff were very relieved by this news!

As often happens, the next generation took what previous generations had started and made it their own. The Millennials demanded even greater flexibility in how and where they do their jobs. As the Millennials move into more managerial roles, they're likely to rewrite the rules even more (and who knows what changes Gen Z will usher in!).

WORK-LIFE BLENDING VERSUS BALANCING

The challenge with the word *balance* is that it implies equal distribution — something that can be difficult (if not impossible) to achieve in areas as time-consuming and complex as work and personal life. The boundary between work and personal life isn't as impermeable as it used to be — something that today's companies and employees are increasingly recognizing. Millennial employees, for example, are drawn to employers who promote a more blended approach to work and life. Millennials "don't mind accessing their work life during their personal life, but they also want to access their personal life during work" — a fact that employers are beginning to recognize as they move away from their policies limiting access to social media and other non-company sites during business hours. According to Chip Espinoza, "Millennials aren't going to turn off their personal lives for eight hours."[6]

Large global companies are particularly at risk for high turnover if they don't respond to the flexibility needs of employees. According to a global-wide study of their 180,000-plus employees (of which two out of three are in their 20s and 30s), consulting firm PwC found that "64 percent of Millennials would like to occasionally work from home, and 66 percent of Millennials would like to shift their work hours." Perhaps more interesting is that across all generations, "15 percent of male employees and 21 percent of female employees would give up some of their pay and slow the pace of promotion in exchange for working fewer hours."[7] Such attitudes present challenges to managers in that an employee who finds a company that offers a work-from-home option or flexible starting hours (even at lower pay) is very likely to leave his or her current company.

Millennials aren't the only ones who want flexibility, though. When Boomers joined the workforce, the concept of work-life balance didn't really exist, but as they start to think about retiring, their attitudes are changing. For many reasons (as discussed in chapter 1), Boomers are extending their working lives. As they age, they're becoming more interested in flexible working arrangements that give them more leisure time while still enabling them to maintain some connection to the office (and their job benefits). If your company has a significant number of Boomers who may be nearing retirement age, one way to avoid an immediate brain drain (and a skills gap) is to talk with your seasoned employees about staying on, but with more flexible working hours or days. Many older employees would jump at the chance to have such an arrangement, which also benefits companies by controlling and staggering departures to make them easier to manage.

PERFORMANCE VERSUS FACE TIME

As an employee, you must understand your boss's point of view: he or she has a list of projects that have to get done, and if they don't, his or her performance will suffer (through withheld raises, missed promotions, and other consequences). Thus, your boss has a vested interest in your getting the job done, and for Gen X and Boomer managers "getting the job done" often equates to seeing employees at their desks every day in the office. Fortunately times are changing, and more seasoned managers are learning how to lighten up on this issue. But the corporate world is still overcoming years of programming on how to lead, so change can be slow—particularly among older managers who, when they entered the workforce long ago, were taught by their managers that showing up every day and being at your desk was part of how you got ahead. That said, savvy managers are trying to figure out what changes they can make to get the best performances from their workers. Their strategies include partnering with employees to establish metrics that actually measure performance and don't just check how many hours an employee spends in the office.

To determine whether employees are productive, managers are increasingly relying on key performance indicators (KPIs). A KPI is a measurement of activity (often called a metric) that indicates how a team, department, or business is performing against its goals. If an activity does not directly influence an employee's achievement of business goals, then it's not a KPI but some other kind of metric. Because KPIs apply only to the most important business goals, not all metrics are KPIs. To establish KPIs, follow this four-step process:

1. Establish for both the short term (6 to 12 months) and the long term (1 year or longer) clear goals that are *critical* to your company, to the mission of your department, or to you personally.
   Example: Increase sales by 20 percent in Product XYZ by year's end while maintaining 20 percent profit margin.
2. Define a limited number of vital success factors needed to reach the goal. What should you focus on to help you get to "done"?
   Examples: Increase market share and market size, improve product quality, decrease reworks, improve customer satisfaction rates.
3. Get specific: add to essential success factors numbers that delineate the parameters of success. Nebulous goals make it harder to determine if a project was successfully completed.
   Examples: Increase market share from $25,000/year to $40,000/year, capture 7.5 percent of a new market, achieve ISO quality certification, decrease rework by 20 percent, achieve highest customer satisfaction rating from *Consumer Reports.*
4. Measure progress: how will you see progress in each critical success factor?
   Examples: In an Excel spreadsheet, label the first column "Start" and in it list the current values of your market share, number of markets, percent complete to ISO certification, present level of rework, and present satisfaction rating. In the second column, list your goals. Use the third column for a comparison period (e.g., three-month intervals, at six months, one year ago).

Once you've established KPIs, share them with your department personnel so everyone on your staff is working toward the same KPIs. Report progress and identify and track the actions that help you get closer to your goals. If you're struggling to determine what KPIs to focus on, think about them from your customers' point of view: what is important to them? Remember, customers can be external (as they are for sales associates) or internal (as they are for service-oriented departments such as HR or facilities).

As a manager, having a rigorous measurement system in place will help you to focus less on where your employees are working and more on the *results* of their actions, which ultimately will reflect well on you and help you keep your Millennial employees engaged. In my 20-plus years of managing managers, I've found that those who have well-defined goals, objectives, and KPIs for their employees focus less on things that don't matter (such as where their employees are sitting) and instead concentrate on empowering and assisting employees in achieving their goals. Whether you're new to management or a veteran manager, setting KPIs should be the foundation of your management approach.

MANAGING FLEXIBILITY

Once you're established goals and KPIs for your employees, it's time to loosen the reins and give them flexibility to determine how and where they achieve those goals. This can be scary, particularly if you've not done flexible working arrangements before. When I first started offering flexible schedules at Oxygen, I typically allowed employees to work from out of the office one day every two weeks. At first I was nervous about implementing this policy, because all of the departments that reported to me were service oriented (facilities, sourcing, security, to name a few), and much of what came our way required in-person assistance. But a lot of paperwork and reports went with those jobs, too, and staff in those departments consistently fell behind on those tasks because they had trouble concentrating in the office. Allowing managers to work from home gave them the head space (and quiet) to take care of their paperwork—and to focus on larger issues and think strategically. Eventually I expanded the policy to let employees work from home largely at their discretion as long as they handled their workloads.

What about employees who don't do reports or manage strategic initiatives? Do they need flexibility, too? Of course they do—because life gets in the way of the best-laid plans. For example, employees who are parents will want time off at some point to attend their children's school activities (and who wants to deny them that joy?). But, it's critical to treat your employees with no children similarly. If they need time off to handle chores such as hair appointments, then let them have it as long as such outings don't interfere with their ability to get their work done (same for the employees who are parents). Just make sure you enact policies that let you measure *performance and accomplishments* not *time in the office*.

If this is all new to you (but something you want to do), before implementing a work-from-home policy, discuss with your employees your expectations for when they are working from out of the office. In the beginning, you may be hypersensitive to any delays in their responses to your e-mails or texts ("Are they blowing off their work?"). Keep in mind, though, that they may be on calls or (as I often do when I need to focus on a task) they may have turned off the ringers on their phones so they can concentrate. Figure out with your employees how you can get in touch with them if something urgent comes up and you need to reach them quickly. Establishing a process for quick communication takes away a lot of the fear associated with someone being out of the office (particularly if you're in a service department). Once you get used to employees working from outside the office, it becomes second nature and not a big deal at all.

Letting employees work from home one day a week isn't the only possible arrangement out there. There are plenty of other ways to give employees flexibility over their schedules:

- *Give a certain number of work-from-home days a year.* Separate from personal days, this is a bank of days that employees can use when they decide they need to work from home. Start out small—say, with four days for six months—and see how that plays out with your employees. As you build up confidence in their ability to still get their jobs done under these circumstances, you can increase the allowance, eventually getting to at least one day a month. (Remember, flexibility is the goal here. One day a month should not be too troublesome for anyone—managers and employees—to handle.)
- *Allow staggered start and end times.* For example, let employees arrive at the office somewhere between 7 a.m. and 9 a.m. and leave between 3 p.m. and 5 p.m. as long as they put in a full eight-hour day. Early birds can be out in time to pick up the kids from school, and people who prefer to sleep in a bit and work later have the option to do so. You may need to coordinate schedules if your team needs to answer phones or provide specific in-person coverage, but employees generally work that out among themselves.
- *Allow split shifts.* In this arrangement, employees work in four-hour increments throughout the day when their services are needed the most. In a call center, for example, if most calls occur during lunch and after the end of the business day, give employees the option to work 11 a.m. to 3 p.m., leave the office for a break, and then return to take calls from the after-work crowd.
- *Allow for a combination of locations.* Let employees combine working from home a certain number of hours each day with putting in hours in the office daily (as long as they keep their calendars updated on their location and availability, so you know how and where to reach them).
- *Allow job sharing.* This option works especially well when two employees in similar positions are both interested in part-time work. In this arrangement, two employees occupy the same position but at different hours. For example, one person might work in the morning and leave a log for the other person who comes in for the afternoon and picks up where the first person left off.
- *Allow compressed work weeks.* If you're managing to KPIs (and not focused on face time), it doesn't matter if the employee is in the office for five eight-hour days or for four ten-hour days.
- *Use technology where possible.* One obstacle to working from home is the inability to access files remotely, so have your IT department set up a virtual private network that lets employees access all the same files as if they were in the office. Teleconferencing and videoconferencing equipment and software can also help employees still "be in the office" a bit even when they work from home (although with the number of free services available, it's more a matter of IT establishing policies than one of rolling out equipment).

- *Adopt a work-from-anywhere policy.* For those positions that truly do not need to be in the office, why not allow workers to work from anywhere as long as they get the job done on time and to your standards? Thus your web developer can work from Hawaii (or the moon), for example, as long as he or she can complete the objectives and be available when needed. This policy has been implemented widely (and with much success) in the tech world, so think outside the box to see how it might work for your field, too.

As you work to develop a more flexible workplace, know that it's usually easier to give flexibility to those employees who consistently provide outstanding performance. Rarely does a top achiever start to underperform because he or she was allowed to come to the office late in order to get the car serviced or get a dental check-up, for example. On the contrary, top performers usually already have the drive and time-management skills needed to handle flexible scheduling responsibly. At the same time, flexible scheduling can also be used to motivate average and subpar performers, because before you let them enjoy that perk they have to prove to you that they're able to get their work done and check in with you frequently when they aren't in the office. Another benefit of flexible scheduling is that it enables top achievers to concentrate better while they're working on company priorities, because the mundane tasks and responsibilities of their personal lives won't be taking away their focus.

In a panel I moderated on work-life balance for a New York Women in Communications event, Jennifer Owens, the editorial director for Working Mother Media, described a winning strategy for any employee who wants to have flexible scheduling: "If you want flexibility, show the boss that you can get the job done regardless of where you're located."[8] Employees who consistently deliver build up trust with their managers and once trust is in place, more good things come their way. It's critical that employees understand that when they're new to an organization, their request to work from home on Fridays, for example, probably won't be approved. But once they demonstrate their capabilities, their managers are more likely to say yes to such a request.

If you do allow flexibility, don't ding your employees when they're back in the office. Don't constantly remind them of the favor you're doing for them by allowing them to work outside the office. If you make your employees feel guilty (or like it's a big deal), chances are they won't work from someplace other than the office because it's too much hassle. You've then defeated your efforts at being a manager who's focused on performance, not on time in the office.

MANAGING VIRTUAL TEAMS

In addition to learning how to offer flexibility to employees in a traditional work setting, you also need to learn how to manage employees who work outside of the office. This skill is particularly critical as the workforce increasingly shifts to a gig economy "in which temporary positions are common and organizations contract with independent workers for short-term engagements."[9] How pervasive is gig work? The percentage of US workers engaged in nontraditional gig work (i.e., work outside the usual 40 hours a week in corporate America) jumped from 10.1 percent in 2005 to 15.8 percent in 2015.[10] According to Intuit, these numbers are expected to climb significantly, with the number of on-demand workers hitting 7.6 million by 2020.[11] With such a forecast, the chance that you'll be managing part-time, contract employees is extremely good, especially as Millennials continue to take over the workforce. A recent national survey found that 38 percent of Millennials freelance—a higher rate than that of other generations.[12] Boomers who wish to continue working past the typical retirement age are also likely to perform gig work. This broad shift to nontraditional corporate jobs means that learning how to manage virtual teams is as critical a skill as being able to manage the direct reports who sit outside your office.

Managing virtual teams is different from managing full-time employees in a flexible environment. In a traditional office setting, your employees are usually in the office at some point during a typical week. As companies shift to part-time or contract workers, however, you may meet just once a year (or even never meet!) with staff members who provide critical services to your department and to the company. Therefore, when leading employees, managers need to be more on point about setting expectations, offering regular coaching sessions, and implementing team-building activities:

- *Establish written goals and objectives.* In previous sections (and chapters) I've discussed the importance of establishing KPIs and goals and objectives at the individual employee level. For those whom you may never meet, it's even more of a necessity, because the lack of face-to-face interaction doesn't allow you to confirm verbally what's due and when (as well as how you need it delivered). For the virtual crowd, *written* goals are a must.
- *Hold weekly team meetings.* Establish regular team meetings, preferably via videoconference or software (such as Google hangout) that allows employees to see one another. (Being able to see their coworkers helps employees build stronger connections with each other—and feel more accountable to each other, too.) Millennials in particular highly value working in teams, so building a team environment will help to keep them engaged and motivated even if they're not sitting in your offices.
- *Send weekly notes.* Set a reminder to send notes regularly (at least once a week) to virtual employees so they know that they matter to you. The notes don't have to be significant—even a quick hello can help foster connectedness among your virtual employees. (As someone who's been doing gig work exclusively for nearly a decade and misses the daily interaction with coworkers in an office environment, I know that these check-in notes can be greatly appreciated!)
- *Be available on a weekly basis.* It can be easy to cancel weekly check-in meetings with employees when you see them every day and you can stop

by their cubicles to chat at any time. With virtual workers, you need to establish (and keep!) a weekly check-in, even if it lasts for just 15 minutes. This is especially critical for Millennial workers (who like lots of feedback), although all employees benefit from these interactions. Regular check-ins demonstrate to the employee that what he or she is working on matters to you and to the company—knowledge that can motivate and engage workers. Check-ins also give employees an opportunity to get any questions they have answered right away (instead of having to wait for your response by e-mail).

- *Encourage informal conversations.* Part of the allure of working in an office is the water cooler chatter that occurs among coworkers. Baby Boomers and Gen Xers in particular enjoy these conversations, because they generally prefer face-to-face interactions. So encourage your virtual team members to pick up their phones and call each other to chat every once in a while.
- *Take time zones into consideration when scheduling calls and meetings.* Because virtual teams can be scattered all across the globe, you may end up with team members in very different time zones. Be sure to take those differences into account when scheduling meetings, and don't make someone always have very early or very late hours just because those times are convenient for you.
- *Be creative with team-building activities.* When working with a team in China for example, I organized a monthly "virtual happy hour" (held at either 6 a.m. or 6 p.m., depending on the participants' time zone) as well as a Hawaiian shirt day (videoconferencing let us admire each other's attire). We also had a "virtual potluck" to which everyone brought a dish. Although we couldn't actually taste each other's food, being able to break bread "together" helped build camaraderie within the team.
- *Be conscious of cultural norms and sensitivities.* Highly motivated employees love to learn new things. If you're managing a team flung across the world, take the opportunity (before beginning a project) to help your employees learn about each other's customs.

NOTES

1. Gogh, Vincent van. Letter to Theo van Gogh. July 23, 1980. http://www .vangoghletters.org/vg/letters/RM25/letter.html.
2. Schawbel, Dan. "Millennial Branding and Beyond.com Survey Reveals the Rising Cost of Hiring Workers from the Millennial Generation." Millennial Branding website. August 6, 2013. http://www.millennialbranding.com/ 2013/cost-millennial-retention-study.
3. PwC. "PwC's NextGen: A Global Generational Study." PwC website. 2013. http://www.pwc.com/gx/en/hr-management-services/pdf/pwc-nextgen-study-2013.pdf.

4. Cambridge Dictionaries Online. *s.v.* "Work-life balance."

5. Devaney, Erik. "Should You Strive for Work/Life Balance? The History of the Personal and Professional Divide." *Hubspot* (blog). July 8, 2015. http://blog.hubspot.com/marketing/work-life-balance.

6. Evans, Lisa. "This Is How Millennials Will Change Management." *Fast Company* online. October 29, 2015. http://www.fastcompany.com/3052617/the-future-of-work/this-how-millennials-will-change-management.

7. PwC. "PwC's NextGen: A Global Generational Study." PwC website. 2013. http://www.pwc.com/gx/en/hr-management-services/pdf/pwc-nextgen-study-2013.pdf.

8. Owens, Jennifer. Comments during "Balancing Work and Family," a panel discussion hosted by New York Women in Communications, New York City. March 8, 2016.

9. Whatis.com. *s.v.* "Gig economy."

10. Katz, Lawrence F., and Alan B. Krueger. "The Rise and Nature of Alternative Work Arrangements in the United States, 1995–2015." Alan B. Krueger's page on the Princeton University website. March 29, 2016. http://krueger.princeton.edu/sites/default/files/akrueger/files/katz_krueger_cws_-_march_29_20165.pdf.

11. Pofeldt, Elaine. "Intuit: On-Demand Workers Will More Than Double by 2020." *Forbes* online. August 13, 2015. http://www.forbes.com/sites/elaine pofeldt/2015/08/13/intuit-on-demand-workers-will-more-than-double-by-2020.

12. Upwork. "53 Million Americans Now Freelance." Upwork website. September 3, 2014. http://www.upwork.com/press/2014/09/03/53-million-americans-now-freelance-new-study-finds-2/.

Chapter 9

MANAGING DIFFERENCES IN CAREER DEVELOPMENT PLANNING

Accomplishments will prove to be a journey, not a destination.
—Dwight D. Eisenhower[1]

Most people want a sense of purpose to their lives—including the time they spend at work. That's why it's so important that managers connect individual employee goals to the organization's mission in order to establish a greater sense of accountability among employees who then feel that they aren't just completing tasks but are setting the company up for future success. But employees want to see that the company is interested in *their* future success as well. After all, if an employee is just punching a clock every day, there's nothing to compel him or her to stay if another opportunity comes along that offers even slightly more money (or other perks).

Enter career development: the secret weapon in every smart manager's toolkit that creates a bond between the company and the manager's direct reports. Employees who see that they have a path to increase their skill sets and move up within an organization are more likely to stay because they can visualize themselves there in the long term. As a manager, you want each employee to feel that his or her position is more than just a job—and that the company is a family in which everyone pulls together to accomplish great things.

Earlier generations haven't always prioritized career planning. Baby Boomers, for example, were raised to believe that they'd stay with the same company for their entire working lives, with their promotions usually doled out based on years of service. Shifts in the global economy, however, made that path less viable for the members of Generation X, who responded by seizing more control over their careers and actively pushed for new opportunities and promotions. On the other end of the spectrum, Millennials grew up believing that they could achieve anything through hard work and relied heavily on their parents, guidance counselors, and teachers to take active roles in shaping their futures. This early team involvement resulted in the expectation that when Millennials entered the workforce, their managers would fill the role of guidance counselor and nurture their career development.

Do these generational differences mean that managers need to focus only on Millennials? Not quite. Creating a career development plan can help you retain high potential employees of any age. The great news? Generation Xers and Boomers may need less coaching on this than Millennials.

EXPECTATIONS OF CAREER DEVELOPMENT BY GENERATION

The generations have widely varying expectations about career development opportunities. When it comes to this subject, one size definitely does not fit all.

So before you develop, adjust, or implement a career development program, make sure it addresses the needs and interests of your employees.

Baby Boomers

The biggest fallacy about Boomers is that their interest in career development ends when they approach the usual age of retirement. True, some may be ready to leave the workforce at that point, but a significant—and growing—number of Baby Boomers actually want to continue working. They don't always want to stay in the full-time positions they've had for decades; for example, some may be interested in phased retirement options or scaling back to less stressful job requirements. However their work situations change (or don't), though, keeping them in the loop on new technologies and innovations will go a long way toward motivating this generation. As with all employees, it's critical to ask for their input about what they want their jobs to be. But since Boomers are from the "just show up and do your work" generation, don't be surprised if they don't know how to answer those questions. So help them out by asking them what new skill sets they want to develop in the next year or two (and then focusing on those that will enrich your department or the company at large). If there isn't a particular position or promotion they want to go after, help them grow in place through training. And don't forget to look at how they can share their extensive experience and expertise with others (perhaps by leading training seminars). No one wants to feel irrelevant, and reminding Boomers that they still have plenty to contribute will increase their job satisfaction and their engagement.

Generation X

It should be somewhat easier to figure out this generation's needs for career development: if you ask a Gen Xer about this subject, he or she will probably lay out a career plan for the next 5 to 10 years. Gen X ushered in the take-charge approach to career development after bearing the brunt of corporate layoffs and feeling a need to seize more control over their careers. Push Gen Xers to think about whether they're keeping pace with industry changes and how those changes correlate to their long-term career plans. Focusing on strategic issues with this group is critical, because these employees are in the prime of their careers. Ensuring that they are out front in their skill sets will go a long way toward reinvigorating their enthusiasm and enticing them to stay with the company longer. This is also a great group to tap for their entrepreneurial abilities and independent spirit. No hand-holding is required for Gen X employees: once you've laid out a career trajectory that spells out the benefits of their jobs, they will be off and running. That doesn't mean you get to dump and run, though—you still need to do regular check-ins on how they're doing against their game plans and offer to help where and when needed. Because this group thrives on being visible, identify career development opportunities (such as presenting to peers and senior leaders) that take advantage of that drive.

Millennials

When you discuss career development with Millennials, keep in mind that for them *career* development also includes *personal* development. Millennials want to find meaning and fulfillment in their everyday work. So ask Millennial employees if their current roles are meeting their personal needs, and if they aren't, figure out what needs to change to make that happen—even if it puts them on a path that leads away from your department. At Oxygen, for example, I allowed my Millennial assistant to help the public relations department with coordinating the company's charitable activities. That work fulfilled her personal needs, and she performed even better at her job in my department. (Eventually, she moved into PR full time and has thrived in that field for the past decade.) Thinking outside the box to expose Millennials to different career options will increase their loyalty to both you and the company. Even though broadening their horizons does mean that some Millennials will spread their wings and leave your organization because you've exposed them to areas they may never have thought of before, they will tell all of their friends (who will tell all of *their* friends) that you're someone who cares about your staff as whole people, not just as employees doing their jobs, and with that reputation, you'll have the cream of the crop flocking to your door. In my entire career, helping others develop their own careers has never been a bad thing.

Generation Z

Generation Z, the newest group of employees to enter the workforce, has many similarities to Millennials and will likewise benefit from exposure to lots of new ideas and opportunities. Arrange for them to have monthly lunches with leaders from other departments (and help them ahead of time to prepare questions to ask), for example, or let them volunteer for projects outside their normal routines. To expose them to organizational strategy, invite them to attend meetings with you. Sign them up to attend company events and give them questions to think about that will help them learn from the experience. For example, if you're attending an awards dinner, "Who is being honored and why?" gets Gen Zers thinking about what hard work is needed to succeed. "What will you say to someone you're seated next to but don't know?" highlights the importance of networking skills, and "How will you introduce yourself and what will you wear?" teaches them about personal brand awareness and first impressions. Company events can be great learning opportunities as long as you follow up with employees afterward to analyze them (and underscore the business aspects at play during the festivities).

USING CAREER DEVELOPMENT FOR SUCCESSION PLANNING AT ALL LEVELS

If you're in the C-suite (CEO, COO, CEO, etc.) chances are you've participated in conversations to identify potential candidates to fill the most senior positions in your company in the event a key leader departs unexpectedly. As necessary as those conversations are, however, it's equally critical to focus on succession planning for the junior ranks, too, because their leadership acumen is the catalyst (or obstacle, when the acumen is lacking) for achieving the vision, mission, and objectives set forth by senior leaders. A proactive approach to career development and managing talent at all levels can ensure a pool of qualified candidates whenever the need arises for additional leadership capabilities. And if you plan well, one of those middle managers may someday be on the short list for a C-suite position.

To Train or Not to Train

In a cartoon that circulated widely a few years ago, one executive says, "What if we train them, and they leave?" and a second one replies, "What if we don't, and they *stay?*"[2] If you've managed employees for even a short amount of time, you've surely encountered this conundrum! Although it's awful when highly trained employees leave (especially if you've invested time and money in their development), it's far worse to have unskilled employees executing your company's vision. When you link succession planning to career development, your employees see opportunities for personal growth and are therefore more likely to remain at your company.

When kicking off career development planning for employees below the senior executive level, consider this two-pronged approach:

1. Identify the critical job functions at the heart of your operations. What skills, knowledge, and abilities are needed to lead these positions?
2. Identify the employees your company should work to keep. Conduct a gap analysis on your high potentials to determine where they are now—and where they need to be to fill the critical positions identified earlier.

Use the gap analysis as the basis for your career development plan, which ties into your succession planning document. Keeping in mind the twin goals of training employees for future responsibilities and honing the skills they need for their current positions, identify what is important now and what is required in the foreseeable future. The most successful development plans typically cover a time frame of one to five years but are still living documents that change as an employee's proficiency in desired skills continues to grow.

Tying Succession Planning to Career Development

Successful succession development involves a formal, individualized plan for each employee—not a one-size-fits-all approach. Standard concepts can be taught in group sessions, but for everything else you need to offer measureable, challenging, and time-bound developmental activities tailored for each person. Some possible activities include:

- Rotational assignments in departments (such as critical production areas) that will increase the employee's knowledge base or in areas where the employee needs development
- Projects that are in line with an employee's current skills yet challenging in some fashion
- Classroom training or case-study analysis, with the results presented to senior management
- Individual coaching or mentoring from either an outside expert or a qualified internal executive
- Coaching and mentoring of other employees in their growth and development
- Specific reading assignments with reports to senior leadership (including discussions of how to use concepts and practices internally)
- Role-playing, with observer feedback
- Shadowing executives

The goal of tying career development to succession planning is to have the right people in the right place at the right time—a goal that applies as much to your middle managers as it does to your senior leaders. Now is the time to start developing talent at *all* levels within your organization.

FIVE EASY STEPS TO CREATING A CAREER PLAN

Creating a career development plan shows employees that you value them not only for the work they're contributing now, but also for what they'll be able to offer the organization in the future (thus strengthening the employee-employer connection). Career planning is empowering for both the employee (because it gives him or her some idea of what the future looks like) and the manager (because it helps direct future training opportunities). There's no downside to creating a career plan for your employees (and don't forget one for yourself, too!). If creating a formal plan is new to you, follow this five-step plan.

Step 1: Start with Company Goals

Any goal-setting activities should start with a review of the company goals. After all, you need to ensure that future growth opportunities for your employees fit into the company's future growth as well (otherwise, all your efforts could be for naught). And don't focus only on your department's growth: thinking in holistic terms that encompass the company at large has the potential to lead to even more opportunities. (A broad perspective is especially important if you don't plan to move to another position in your company and, therefore, end up blocking those below you.) Based on your company's short- and long-term business objectives, identify the competencies and skill sets that are needed to reach those goals.

Step 2: Involve Your Employees

My best piece of advice when it comes to creating career development plans for your employees is to *not* assume that you know their aspirations. Have a face-to-face discussion (or a videoconference, if you manage remote employees and cannot meet in person) with all of your direct reports to understand what career goals they have for themselves. Ask for their reasons for those goals, too, because if your company doesn't have particular positions that they want, you may be able to find some other way to fulfill the *why* behind their goals.

Some employees (especially those new to the workforce, such as Millennials or Gen Zers) might not have specific career goals in mind and don't know how to figure those out. So talk with them about what they like—and don't like— about their current jobs. Ask them questions that will help them focus on their long-term goals. What do they wish they could do more (or less) of in their day-to-day work? What career ambitions did they have when they first entered the workforce? (That's a great question to ask employees of any age, not just younger ones.) What skill sets do they want or need to work on?

Another reason not to assume that you know an employee's career goals is that he or she may not have long-term ambitions in your department but may instead favor other areas in your company. At Oxygen Media, I worked with my senior director of operations to create a career plan that put him in line to replace me. When he went back to school for a master's degree in a completely different field, his career objectives changed—and our plan had to change, too. I proactively pushed for a transfer for him to a different department more in line with his new interests to give him a new career path (thus helping the company keep a great employee) and upon his departure, I promoted his second-in-command to his post (thus expanding *her* career growth opportunities). Fortunately, this turned out to be a win-win situation for everyone. I share this story with new managers to highlight how tough it can be to manage employees—and how rewarding it can be to help them succeed professionally.

Step 3: Decide What Competencies Are Missing

Once you've looked at your company's short- and long-term objectives and had a conversation with your employees about what they're looking to do with their careers, it's time to see how their goals line up with what they're doing in their day-to-day jobs and where your employees need improvement. What skill sets do each of your employees need to improve upon in order to meet the future needs of your company?

Step 4: Create an Action Plan

Now it's time to get serious and create an action plan with specific SMART goals (see chapter 4 for more details), including a time frame for completion and a rubric for measuring improvement. With such a plan in place, your employees can track their performance so there won't be any surprises when it's time to discuss their progress. This is also the point at which you and your employees figure out which activities (training, job-shadowing, coaching, etc.) will best help the employee improve. In essence, this is the fun part!

Step 5: Monitor, Measure, and Make Adjustments as Needed

A career development plan is a living, breathing document. So if you decided on a training methodology that's not working, no worries—stop doing it and find something else. Making adjustments is an expected part of the process, and ideally it takes place before you've spent too much time and money going down the wrong path. Once a plan is formulated, your continued involvement in your employees' career growth is key: at a minimum, meet with them individually once a month (Millennials may want more frequent check-ins) to discuss their progress, and, if they aren't moving forward, provide the feedback and coaching they need to get back on track.

CREATING A COMPANY-WIDE DEVELOPMENT PROGRAM SPECIFIC TO LEADERSHIP

In conversations with your employees about their future career goals, obtaining a position of leadership is one topic that will inevitably come up (and may even be the first one out of your employee's mouth). Leadership skill is challenging to cultivate, and great leaders are in short supply. But it's worth taking the time to identify and encourage leadership potential in your employees. So if your company does not already have a formal leadership development program (LDP), consider creating one that works both for employees and for your company. Rather than wait for leaders to knock on your door, *make your own leaders*. By building on the potential and drive of your current employees, you'll ensure the success of your department and organization now and in the future.

Determining What Matters

Before looking for potential candidates in your organization, first define what competencies are critical in a great leader at your company. What does it take to be a great leader in your organization? Competencies can vary by level (e.g., front-line supervisor, mid-level manager, senior executive) and perhaps by business unit. In most organizations, however, fundamental competencies apply across the board. At the most senior levels, a great leader typically exhibits the following attributes (or some variation of this group):

- Visionary
- Inspirational
- Strategic
- Tactical
- Persuasive
- Decisive
- Ethical

Notice this list does not necessarily denote technical skills. Rather, it highlights a leader's ability to understand and process new information, make decisions (often before all the details are available), translate those decisions or visions into action, and then rally the troops to get on board. Technical mastery may be found on the leadership spectrum, but it certainly should not be the only criteria for leadership within your company (even if your company is technical in nature).

Your first step toward developing your LDP is to determine what matters most at your company. This knowledge will then allow you to compare your employees' current skills with the skills your company needs.

Identifying Candidates

Some programs allow employees to apply to participate in LDPs, whereas others specifically pick candidates who have been identified as high-potential employees. Regardless of how applicants come to you, you'll need to define the selection criteria by which you'll evaluate them. One easy-to-identify factor is how much supervisory experience an employee has. Other key criteria include traits such as the ability to learn new things, an interest in leading (don't assume that everyone wants to be a leader!), the ability to engage in teamwork eagerly and effectively, a high confidence level, and any skills that are in alignment with the organization's future direction and growth. General intelligence is also important, but it's not the only trait that guarantees success in a leadership role.

A numeric rating system (a scale of 1 to 5, for example) is helpful for aggregating and comparing input from multiple executive leaders. In addition to giving you an at-a-glance view of any candidate you're considering for an LDP, it also allows the opinions of less verbose leaders to carry as much weight as those from reviewers who campaign vigorously on behalf of their candidates.

Assessing Current Leadership Skills

Once you've established the competencies important for your organization and selected the participants for your LDP, it's time to measure each employee's existing skill set against what he or she needs to have in order to be a great leader in your organization. Performance appraisals and 360-degree leadership surveys are just a couple of the powerful measurement tools at your disposal. Another method to assess current skill levels is to have participants answer a series of essay questions on how they would tackle certain problems built around the critical competencies you've identified. Their responses to each scenario can help identify specific skills they lack.

You can also devise simulation activities that highlight an employee's ability to plan, organize, make decisions, and lead programs. Involving your senior leadership team in creating these activities can be a great learning exercise on its own (and sharpen the leadership skills of your current executives). If you have money to spend, consider hiring an outside company to conduct observation-based assessments of your staff's current skill levels.

Developing Employees' Skills

Once you've identified the skills you need, it's time to develop them and take your employees' abilities to the next level. In his article "Creating a Leadership Development Program," Robert Pernick wrote that leadership development typically occurs in three related areas:

> *Technical*—enhances the skills needed to perform work or to oversee the work of others
> *Conceptual*—based on thinking in a more abstract and critical fashion (this is connected to creativity, strategic thinking, and decisiveness)
> *Interpersonal*—related to the ability to work effectively with other people[3]

Although thought exercises and role-playing are useful training methods, whenever possible leaders should receive their training while dealing with actual on-the-job issues. Real life—and real consequences—can motivate high-potential employees to succeed. That said, it's important to understand that leaders-in-training can and may fail. Rather than crucify these young leaders for their mistakes, push them to learn from failures and to apply their hard-won knowledge to future challenges.

It's critical to put all the parts of an employee's career development plan into writing. Unless goals, time lines, and measurement rubrics are carefully documented, the plan doesn't really exist.

Assessing Progress

Your performance evaluation systems should support employee development in the competencies you've defined as critical to your organization. In short, they need to make it possible for you to connect what you're teaching with what you're measuring. Six months after you launch your LPD (and then at, say, 6- or 12-month intervals moving forward), reevaluate your employees according to the same criteria that were originally used to assess their pre-LDP skill sets. Consistent and thorough assessments will reveal whether your employees are making progress.

CREATING YOUR OWN CAREER DEVELOPMENT PLAN

Although most managers recognize the importance of creating career development programs for their employees, many (many!) managers either don't know how or won't take the time to create career development for *themselves*. Don't be one of those managers! Take the time to figure out what you want in your career and how to get it.

The path to greater responsibilities can be built only on a solid foundation. So before you begin planning your promotion, be sure you're performing at the highest level in your present position. Once you've reached that apex, you can then focus on the position you desire and your plan for getting there. I once worked with an extraordinary executive coach, Gloria Henn, who urged me to think of leadership as a pie, with each slice representing a different skill set. As a person's responsibilities change throughout his or her career, he or she needs to master the skills needed to rise to the new challenge A great leader has more slices completed (you'll never achieve 100%, because there is always something new to learn), so start the creation of your career development plan by asking yourself what skills (or slices of pie) are needed for the position you want, and paying careful attention to which ones you don't already have.

In addition to the attributes described earlier, a good leader may (depending on his or her particular position) need expertise in these areas as well:

- Technical skills
- Industry knowledge
- Negotiation skills
- Ability to delegate effectively
- Willingness and ability to take ownership and responsibility

Compare the desired attributes and skills with your competencies, then work with your boss to identify the ones that are most critical to the position you seek. (Asking your boss for advice may get him or her more involved in your career development, too.) At some point, you may end up asking your boss for funding for your training (or to give you a promotion, when you master the skills you need!), so it's prudent to keep him or her in the know as you create your own leadership development plan.

Getting Honest Feedback

Once you've identified which slices of pie you need and start to work toward your goals, you'll need to measure your progress. But it is very difficult (if not impossible) to be objective about oneself. To increase the accuracy of your self-assessment, therefore, solicit feedback from your employees and colleagues. That's easier said than done, though: for a host of reasons, it can be difficult for both direct reports and peers to speak honestly about a supervisor or coworker. To help alleviate any potential discomfort surrounding this situation, it's critical to be open-minded about receiving feedback and suspend your judgment of what they tell you. And it's especially critical to control your defensiveness, because coworkers often fail to provide useful assessments when they have to spend more time defending that information than actually giving the feedback to the employee. (And anyone who's ever been put in that position usually resolves never to give feedback to a coworker again, even if he or she begs for it!) Instead, receive the feedback in a positive, encouraging manner that will invite more feedback. Listen closely, ask clarifying questions, and take notes to understand where your coworkers think your skills need improvement. If possible, get feedback from at least five (more, if you can) people. Those assessments of you that are widely held are more likely to be accurate and need to be addressed. Those that have a low frequency may be wrong and should, at the very least, be considered with caution.

If your company offers 360-degree performance evaluations, which gather feedback from one's immediate work circle (including peers, superiors, and subordinates), sign up for one immediately! This valuable tool offers excellent feedback, partly because it includes a wide range of participants and partly because its inherent anonymity allows participants to give more honest feedback. (Don't try to associate comments with specific individuals—that defeats the point of getting anonymous feedback!) If your company does not offer 360-degree performance evaluations, you can create your own versions of them through online survey companies. For an approach that's more low-tech (but just as effective), you can distribute a survey as a Word document and ask respondents to submit their completed forms electronically to a neutral party who can remove identifying information (e.g., e-mail headers) before passing them over to you, or ask them to leave printouts of their responses in your office mailbox. To ensure that your questions and wording do not breach any company policies, it's best to involve your HR representative or your boss when generating questions. Including your boss can also highlight you as a motivated go-getter seeking to improve your skills on your own in the absence of a formal system through the company.

Identifying Training Opportunities

Once you've identified what you need to work on, speak with your boss about potential on-the-job training opportunities, such as taking on a rotational assignment in another department or office, spearheading a project in an area in which you need improvement, or shadowing your boss or another executive. Establishing a formal coaching or mentoring relationship with an executive other than your boss (either inside or outside your organization) can be another great way to expand both your education and the career options available to you.

Numerous LDP-oriented classroom training options exist, but if your company is unable or unwilling to pay for one, you can put together your own course of study. For example, you can download case studies or books to read and discuss with your fellow executives. A great way to start compiling your reading list is to ask your boss and C-level executives what books have been particularly inspirational or useful in their development. Perhaps you can start your own book club at the office and ask the executive who recommended a particular book to lead the discussion on it.

Online training is another route to gaining additional leadership experience, as is volunteering for a nonprofit group, school organization, or community-based program. In addition to expanding your skill set, volunteering can also expand your network of contacts (which is *never* a bad thing!).

Staying on Track

Obviously, it's easier to stay on track if you're involved in a company LDP plan that structures and monitors your progress. But if you're on your own, you'll have to work hard to avoid getting buried in your day-to-day responsibilities and to keep your focus on developing your leadership skills. Once you've established specific objectives and a time line for achieving them, add milestones so you can recognize—and celebrate—your progress along the way. Remember, too, that much of what we do in life is habitual, so work to create good habits that will enable you to work toward your goals with both greater ease and greater success. Be sure to record your progress systematically, in a journal, in your online calendar, or in whatever works for you so you can easily see what you've accomplished—and what you need to improve—and stay engaged with the overall project.

NOTES

1. Eisenhower, Dwight D. "Remarks at the Opening of the NATO meetings in Paris." December 16, 1957. http://www.presidency.ucsb.edu/ws/?pid=10962.

2. This cartoon has circulated widely—without any attribution—on the Internet for several years. (A search for "corporate dilemma investing in employees cartoon" turns up hundreds of hits.) The original source of this cartoon is unknown.

3. Pernick, Robert. "Creating a Leadership Development Program: Nine Essential Tasks." *Public Management* 84 (August 2002): 10–17.

Chapter 10

GENERATIONAL GIVE AND TAKE

There was no respect for youth when I was young, and now that I am old, there is no respect for age—I missed it coming and going.

The biggest challenge in a multigenerational workplace is dealing with conflict among the generations. Employees of any age rarely appreciate what other generations have to offer and instead approach each other with preconceived notions about how an employee of a certain age behaves. Baby Boomers think Millennials are know-it-alls, Millennials think Baby Boomers have no new ideas, and the members of Generation X believe that no one works as hard as they do and that they are the best leaders of any generation. The old dismiss the young for not having enough experience, while the young dismiss the old for being obsolete. Rather than try to bridge the generational gap, employees tend to hunker down in their respective age silos, which only serves to increase tension in the office among employees of varying ages. No wonder a clash of generations typically ensues.

In order for a multigenerational workplace to be an environment in which people can work effectively and harmoniously, employees (and particularly managers) must set aside any prejudices they have about their coworkers and appreciate all generations for the skills they bring to the office. Otherwise, each interaction will only widen the gap further, thus killing productivity. The first time a Millennial presents an idea and gets "No, we've already done that" in response, the gap widens into a chasm, because the younger employee feels shut down by the seasoned staff. In that same interaction, the veteran staffer who's already presented that same idea on other occasions (perhaps numerous times) is annoyed that a Millennial thinks no one was smart enough to come up with that idea before. (And when something feels like a personal slight, it's no surprise that more seasoned employees are inclined to respond negatively to it.) This vicious cycle repeats itself every time someone opens his or her mouth unless everyone makes a conscious effort to value what others bring to the work-place: younger employees need to view their more seasoned peers as experienced veterans with a lifetime of knowledge to share, and older employees must learn to regard their younger colleagues as those who need guidance, not condescension (since they will one day run the company—and the economy at large). Embracing an attitude of mutual respect is the only way to guarantee the company's future. Remember, you're all in this together—and will succeed or fail together.

COMMUNICATION IS KEY

As with most problems in the office, miscommunication is often a likely culprit when tensions mount among coworkers. The rise in the use of written communication (e-mail, text, IM, etc.) in the workplace has not helped the situation, because tone can be hard to gauge (and easy to misinterpret) in those media. Age differences further compound the problem: communication can be challenging enough among participants of the same age, let alone among employees who are two, three, or even more decades apart.

Further problems can arise when the age gap exists not just between employees but also between employees and supervisors. As more and more Millennials step into management roles, they often find themselves supervising workers who are a generation (or more) older than them. And unfortunately, many companies do not offer management training, which further aggravates an already challenging situation when new managers are decades younger than their direct reports. These freshly minted managers have to remember that they're not communicating with their parents, even if their direct reports are the same age as their parents (or even their grandparents!). Younger managers need to be able to provide feedback effectively to somebody who's older than they are.

Older managers (even those with extensive experience as supervisors), too, need to be aware of and address communication challenges that can arise in interactions with younger employees. Even when everyone is speaking the same language, slang and vocabulary can make it difficult for members of different generations to understand each other. For example, Millennials often use terms that are inspired by new technologies (and popularized through social media) and that few people older than 30 understand. Although an older manager doesn't have to be fluent in "Millennialese" when coaching younger employees, it is important that he or she have some understanding of what motivates and engages them. It's also critical that an older manager refrain from treating younger employees as if they were his or her children.

THE HOW AND WHEN OF COMMUNICATION

One of the biggest shifts I've seen in the more than two decades I've spent in corporate America is the change in communication media. When I was in my 20s, if I wanted to communicate with people from work I actually had to pick up a phone and call them or go visit them. When I was given a pager in 1989, I felt like I was "somebody"; the first time it went off, I stood up and announced to all my friends that I had to go make a phone call immediately because someone urgently needed to get in touch with me. Today, instead of pager beeping we hear cell phone ringtones, text pings, and other noisy alerts. We no longer have to run to find phones when our devices beep, but instead have become slaves to our mobile devices and the e-mail, texts, and phone calls they deliver to us. Technology is changing at such a rapid pace that it's impossible to predict what the main way to communicate will be even just a few years from now.

As younger generations continue to usher in new methods for communicating with one another, it's important for older generations (especially those in management and leadership positions) to keep up with the changes. It wasn't too long ago that the members of Generation X had to persuade Baby Boomers to embrace e-mail in favor of phone calls and faxes. Just two decades later, many Millennials see e-mail as old-fashioned, preferring instead to use newer media, such as texting and cloud-based collaboration tools, for work communication.

Whatever newer communication methods your company prefers, you need to make sure that every employee is comfortable using them. At the same time, though, keep in mind the needs of older employees (in particular, members of Generation X and Baby Boomers) who may not be as adept with new technologies. So don't abandon "older" forms of communication, such as:

- Telephone message blasts
- Intranet announcements
- E-mail
- PowerPoint presentations
- In-person meetings
- Flyers
- Video

In order to reach younger employees (especially Millennials and members of Generation Z), keep expanding the options to include newer, more social forms of communication, such as:

- Company blogs
- Text messaging
- Twitter or Facebook campaigns
- Niche social networking sites applicable to your industry
- Podcasts
- Interactive webinars
- RSS (Rich Site Summary) feeds
- Live video streams (such as Facebook Live, Periscope, or Meerkat)
- Recorded videos posted online (on sites such as YouTube, Vine, or Snapchat)
- Other cloud-based sharing software (such as Slack, for example)

Employing a variety of communications methods will ensure that your message is heard (and heard correctly, if you're consistent across platforms).

To help keep employees of all ages current on new technologies in the workplace, consider implementing a reverse mentoring program in which younger employees teach their colleagues about the latest offerings. As president of the New York chapter of Women in Cable Telecommunications, I introduced such a program into that organization's Tech It Out series, which used demonstrations and training to keep our members current on the latest technology trends and innovations. Our Millennial-led sessions covered Periscope, Meerkat, Snapchat, Venmo, Slack, and other similar technologies. Through this program, young and old employees alike had opportunities to try new things and expand their skill sets.

Reverse mentoring also lets more senior workers see firsthand how working with younger employees can help them stay current in their own positions. Younger members enjoy the opportunity to switch roles and teach their older peers, while seasoned professionals get to pick up new skills that allow them to stay in touch with the rest of the workplace. Because many veteran workers fear becoming obsolete, the knowledge and new tech skills they gain at these sessions can help them continue to feel relevant—and be even more valuable to their employers.

It's important to evaluate not only *how* workplace communication happens but also *when* it happens. Millennials tend to place a high value on work-life balance and for that reason are more likely than their predecessors to push back if an exorbitant number of hours (beyond the normal 40) are required on a routine basis. Many Baby Boomers and members of Generation X, on the other hand, have had jobs in which they were expected to deal with work-related matters in the evening and on weekends. Different generations have different expectations about how available employees (and managers) should be outside the office. So it's important that leaders and workers make sure they are on the same page for these matters, so that perceptions of too much—or not enough—communication don't lead to other problems.

It's also important to remember that different generations have different expectations about how often communication should take place. Millennial employees tend to expect more feedback than Generation Xers, and Baby Boomers usually prefer very little. Thus a Millennial manager might find it unusual that older employees are able to work independently, hardly ever seeking feedback and generally providing updates only when asked. Baby Boomers in particular are quite often content to take on a project, fall off management's radar for a few weeks, and then report back with final results when they've finished everything. Millennials, on the other hand, prefer to have multiple check-ins throughout the process. They're also accustomed to being more involved in making decisions that affect them, in part because their parents have solicited their input since they were born ("What do you want for dinner?" and "Where should we go on our family vacation?" for example). That's why simply giving orders to Millennials can alienate them—and why brainstorming sessions can get them as excited and engaged as the next iPhone release.

Effective communication among managers and employees of any age can exist only when they share their expectations with each other. The manager sets the tone, though. If he or she makes it clear that monthly check-ins are expected for a yearlong project, for example, then team members know what they need to do—and that any behavior outside of those parameters could create tension or other problems. Differences in communication styles are often heightened when age gaps come into play, but clearly expressed guidelines will help a manager avoid such generational culture clashes.

APPRECIATING THE CONTRIBUTIONS OF YOUTH

During a training class I conducted for a client in Seattle, a Millennial employee vented to me that what she heard most often from older workers was "No, we can't do it." She was frustrated by their apparent lack of openness to new ideas, particularly in one situation in which her proposed solution to an existing problem was initially shot down in this manner but was later adopted after further discussion within the department. This is an all-to-common scenario in which the initial no from older workers is not so much a rejection of an idea but a rejection of how a younger worker has presented it. Such conflict arises not only from differences in age but from differences in tenure, too: a recent hire might enter a workplace ready to turn the system around, only to have his or her ideas shot down by long-term employees who've been at the company for years.

Seasoned employees need to be more open to ideas and appreciate the enthusiasm that young employees and new hires bring to the table instead of outright rejecting their suggestions (even if those ideas have been tried before). Because they're new to the workforce, everything is still exciting to them. Remember feeling fresh and being eager to contribute when you first joined the workforce or your organization? Chances are you often came up with lots of great new ideas—just as Millennials do today.

Sometimes all that's needed to reveal a solution to an existing problem is a new perspective and some perseverance. Just because an idea has already been explored doesn't mean all possible approaches have been exhausted. Consider the example of Thomas Edison, who supposedly quipped, "Many of life's failures are people who did not realize how close they were to success when they gave up" just a few years before he finally succeeded (after several hundred—or, by some accounts, several thousand—failed attempts) in creating a long-lasting lightbulb.

When a younger worker expresses an idea that has already been explored, instead of dismissing the proposal with a "Been there, done that" response, the more seasoned employee should instead try to analyze it in light of past approaches. Discussing prior efforts, sharing documentation of them (such as reports and e-mail), and pointing the younger employee to those who've worked on the problem before can yield fresh perspectives that might enable the office's new blood to see a way around obstacles that stymied others in the past. After all, if an idea was great when it was first brought up, why not help someone else finally figure out a way to achieve that goal? The worst that can happen is the idea fails again. But in the best-case scenario, everyone involved—both the new employee and the veteran—comes out smelling like roses.

By not killing ideas immediately and instead providing support for them, you can encourage younger workers to keep coming up with those new ideas—and even mistakes can often lead to completely new solutions. For example, Post-its were developed when a 3M chemist's attempts to create a super-strong adhesive resulted instead in the weaker yet reusable glue that eventually allowed those little yellow rectangles to become ubiquitous in the office.[2] Remember the big picture, in which the company's success is the end goal. Fostering new ideas and new strategies for achieving that goal will help ensure the organization's longevity for years to come.

If you hear your workers respond, "That can't be done" right off the bat when hearing a new employee's ideas, step in and encourage an open dialogue that transforms "That can't be done" into "That might be possible—but be prepared to encounter the following roadblocks with this approach." You'll not only better equip everyone for success but also come across as an approachable, sensible leader who inspires employees. Of course, not every idea can be pursued (for lack of resources, financing, or staffing, among other reasons). But when you must reject a younger employee's proposal, be sure to explain clearly the reasoning behind the decision so that person can be better prepared the next time he or she presents an idea.

VALUING THE WISDOM OF AGE

At the same time, younger employees also need to learn how to see things from the perspectives of their more seasoned colleagues. In some cases, for example, a workplace veteran might take a suggestion as a personal affront by the younger coworker: the older worker thinks that the younger one assumes that no one has thought of that idea before. This often happens when younger workers enthusiastically present their great solutions for problems without taking into consideration the older employees' experience (and the fact that they may have also tried to tackle those problems themselves).

Should older workers be less sensitive? Of course. (In fact, it would be great if everyone stopped taking things so personally!) But look at the situation from their point of view: they (like everyone else) want to be valued for their experience and what they bring to the table. Taking the approach of enlisting help from all team members (regardless of age) means welcoming all input—and finding value even in the negative stuff. After all, knowing what's been tried without success before may cut down on the time spent to find a winning solution on the next go-around. Encourage employees to treat a no as an opportunity to understand their colleagues' objections and therefore make their pitches even stronger the next time.

If you're the Millennial who's pitching new ideas, don't get offended when someone (of any age) tells you no. Instead, ask for more information about why something can't be done. If an older employee responds, "We already tried it," push for more information about past efforts. Treat the experience as an opportunity to learn about how the problem was approached in the past so that you don't waste your time repeating a failed methodology and end up with the same result.

As you pitch ideas for improving operations, keep in mind that someone who's currently in your company (or even your group) may be the person who implemented the practices you're trying to change. Criticizing an idea while suggesting an alternative that you think is better may incense him or her to the point of being unable to listen to new ideas. That actually happened to me when I was in my late 20s and had just joined the R&D marketing department at Rolls-Royce. At the time, the department used an antiquated Excel spreadsheet to track customers, and I proposed switching to the much better customer relationship management (CRM) system that I had used in another department—and I made some incredibly derogatory comments about the Excel-based system. It turned out that my boss was the one who had rolled out the Excel form. He was so irritated by my comments that he rejected my idea outright without even letting me get into the details of it, and there was tension on both sides: I felt rebuffed and slighted, while he felt that his toes had been stepped on.

Fortunately, my boss was an outstanding mentor: rather than deride my actions during that meeting, he taught me to leave personal judgments out of my professional presentations and instead to focus on how my new ideas can help the company achieve its goals. That's a lesson of value to employees and managers of all ages. Everyone needs to learn how to avoid emotional reactions during business discussions and keep the conversation centered on problem solving—an approach that will yield great results.

PROMOTING POSITIVE INTERACTIONS

Managers who seek to create an inclusive environment should make sure that new (and even not-so-new) ideas are not summarily dismissed. Everyone—young and old—needs to be treated with respect, and that means giving their recommendations serious consideration regardless of how they are presented. Could younger workers present their ideas in ways that are less irritating to their older coworkers? Of course. At the same time, older workers should avoid immediately shooting down ideas brought up by their younger colleagues. A professional demeanor during presentations is certainly preferred, but when someone's in the grip of unbridled enthusiasm for an idea, a respectful tone might inadvertently (and temporarily) fall by the wayside—particularly with younger workers who lack familiarity with office rules and politics. In these situations, workforce veterans should remember that they likely exhibited similar behavior early in their careers. Rather than deal out harsh criticism they should take it upon themselves to step in to offer guidance, a simple gesture that can go a long way toward bridging the generation gap.

Whenever conflict arises over the presentation of new ideas in the workplace, chances are good that some failure of communication is at the root of the problem. When the parties involved are from different generations—and therefore have different life and work experiences—it's critical that they all pay careful attention to what they say, how they say it, and how someone else might hear those words. With practice, employees of any age can learn how to be more sensitive to such communication nuances in the workplace. The following two sample conversations offer some ideas on how to handle (including what not to say) some typical workplace scenarios.

Example 1

Counterproductive conversation

Younger/new employee: "Why are we still doing annual performance reviews? This process is so antiquated and not timely enough."

Older/veteran employee (perhaps the one who originally rolled out the "antiquated" process): "It gets the job done. There's no sense fixing something that isn't broken."

Productive conversation

Younger/new employee: "I know the company has done annual performance reviews for years, but I've heard of some solutions that are more efficient and can help improve performance quicker. Could I do some research and get back to you on how we could improve our current process?"

Older/veteran employee: "That sounds great! I would love to know about the more current options that could help us be more efficient and be more helpful to managers. How do you propose starting this process?"

Example 2

Counterproductive conversation

Younger/new employee: "Why don't we have peanut butter ice cream on the menu? It's the new, hip flavor. We look old-fashioned not having it."

Older/veteran employee: "We tried that flavor a while back, and it didn't work out."

Productive conversation

Younger/new employee: "You may have already tried this, but what if we added peanut butter ice cream to the menu? If you've already tried it, how did it go?"

Older/veteran employee: "We tried that flavor a while back. Many customers liked it, but it also scared off lots of other customers who have peanut allergies. Do you have any suggestions for how we could offer peanut butter ice cream while making sure we didn't contaminate the other flavors? And ideas for how to let our allergic customers know they can enjoy our other flavors without worry?"

In the productive conversations, an idea is presented in a manner that leads to conversation and not to a flat-out rejection. It's also presented without judgment, so that other participants aren't put on the defensive.

At the moment a practice or policy is put in place, it's usually the best option available. Over time, though, circumstances, needs, and options change, so all programs need to be reviewed periodically to make sure they're still relevant and useful. Eventually, it's necessary to try something new—a realization that may be more evident to someone who's looking at a situation for the first time than to someone who's been looking at it for years. Younger employees bring a new perspective to the table, and older employees can take inspiration from that perspective. So instead of shutting down younger employees' ideas, enlist their help with developing better ones. As health-care management expert Mark Graban points out, "Bad managers tell employees what to do, good managers explain why they need to do it, but great managers involve people in decision making and improvement."[3] So be a great manager and invite employees of all ages to participate in the idea-creation process.

THE CHALLENGE OF THE YOUNG LEADING THE WISE

Although older workers still dominate management, younger employees are taking on more and expanded roles in the workforce. And although the Baby Boomers are approaching the age at which employees traditionally leave work to enjoy their golden years, that generation is changing the nature of retirement. Many of today's would-be retirees don't want to simply stop working and go off into the sunset. Instead, they're tapering off slowly, with many opting to work shorter hours in lieu of quitting cold turkey. But with those shorter hours comes the need to hand over the management reins, often to younger and younger managers.

Both sides should see this shift as a golden opportunity. For older employees, it means less stress, more leisure time, and the chance to pass on years of accumulated wisdom. For the young managers stepping into their predecessors' shoes, it means increasing their knowledge more quickly, which in turn enables them to climb the corporate ladder even faster.

It isn't a new thing for young managers to supervise older employees. Always hungry for new ideas, companies have often turned to new graduates and fresh blood for inspiration and innovation. At the age of 24, I supervised a 52-member, all-male, facilities-maintenance crew at Allison Gas Turbine (a division of General Motors that was later sold to Rolls-Royce). As I've grown older, the percentage of older employees on my teams has, naturally, grown smaller (though I've rarely had a job that didn't involve managing at least a few employees older than me).

When I started at Allison, I knew that the situation would be difficult if I went in with the wrong mind-set. I couldn't teach my team members anything about how to do their jobs better, because they were already top-notch experts in their fields. But since my strength lay in analyzing money and time (two highly variable resources at any company), within a month of starting my new job I made it a point to ask each employee to tell me what five tools he needed to get his work done more easily and more efficiently. I found many similarities among the lists and focused my efforts on securing those items as quickly as possible. Through this experience I gained my team's trust by asking their opinions, and they learned that even though I couldn't help them perform routine maintenance or do asbestos removal, I could make their daily workload more bearable, which was something that was otherwise out of their control. I figured out where I, as a new employee, could contribute and helped improve the efficiency of my department of seasoned veterans (and, in turn, helped improve my employees, myself, and our company).

Not all new managers are able to come up with ideas for facilitating a smooth transition. Sometimes they need a little help to make things a bit less bumpy as they try to forge new relationships with their (older) staff. Executives who place younger employees in management roles over older employees can defuse a potentially tense situation by openly addressing the leadership change and helping build bridges between the generations. For example, discuss with each employee ahead of time what he or she brings to the table and share that information with the new manager. This exercise is particularly important for older workers, who want to be valued for both their past contributions and the ones they will continue to make in the future. It sets the stage for both sides to feel comfortable in the new arrangement: the current employees are assured of their value, and the new manager gains valuable information about each team member's strengths.

NOTES

1. Priestley, J. B. Source unknown. Used by kind permission of the J. B. Priestley Estate.
2. Glass, Nick, and Tim Hume. "The 'Hallelujah Moment' behind the Invention of the Post-It Note." CNN online. April 4, 2013. http://www.cnn.com/2013/04/04/tech/post-it-note-history/.
3. Graban, Mark. "What Bad Managers, Good Managers, and Great Managers Do." LinkedIn. September 15, 2014. http://www.linkedin.com/pulse/2014091 1010334-81312-what-bad-managers-good-managers-and-great-managers-do/.

Chapter 11

YOU AS THE MOTIVATING FORCE

Always do what you are afraid to do.

—Ralph Waldo Emerson[1]

Managing people is tough. And being a *good* manager is even tougher, particularly because most managers today are pulling double duty—managing direct reports while also carrying projects of their own because staff levels have been so reduced. If you're new to managing employees, after reading this far you may be thinking to yourself "What have I gotten myself into?" Even if you're not a new manager, you may be thinking similar thoughts. In fact, *all* managers have those doubts and anxieties at some point. (In more than two decades of managing, I've asked myself that question at least once a year!) Being a manager today is more challenging than it's ever been. Every employee requires a personal development plan rivaling an NFL team's playbook in complexity. And long gone are the days where management could ask an employee to do a task, and she or he would do it without question. Now you need to provide the why, how, and where before your employees will start to tackle the project! It's a brave new world out there, and even if you have been incredibly successful at managing employees for many years, it's time to update your style to meet the needs of your Millennials while motivating all generations to come together as a team for continued success.

EXPECTATIONS OF TODAY'S MANAGER

When I first started managing employees (in the early 1990s), my two main responsibilities were identifying potential roadblocks that would affect the schedule and providing financial oversight to ensure the team met budgetary restrictions. My project management skills were put to the test as I focused on ensuring that my employees had the tools and instructions they needed to complete their jobs. This experience was a great way for me to break into being a manager, because my group was already very self-motivated and had effective routines for getting projects accomplished, so I could then work on adding value and engaging and motivating them. Managing employees isn't always such smooth sailing, though. More than ever before, today's managers need to be able to wear a variety of hats:

- *Psychologist*—To be a good manager, you need to be able to understand the wants and desires of your employees, and then put into practice motivational techniques that connect to those inner feelings. You also need to be intuitive, picking up if something is wrong and your employee needs more support with specific projects.

- *Forensic accountant*—As you move to a management role, chances are you'll have budgetary responsibilities. Unfortunately, most companies don't provide financial training and usually assume that managers already have that knowledge. Whether or not you are a finance expert, you'll certainly be held accountable if you or your employees mishandle money.
- *Head coach*—Employees constantly need to hear that they're doing a good job and to "keep up the good work." Inspiration is no longer intrinsic—it's now up to the manager to provide a steady stream of encouragement to help employees feel motivated to do their jobs. And if your pep talks are ineffective, you'll constantly be recruiting for your team, because few employees will stick around
- *Mob enforcer*—Cajoling and nudging will get you only so far. At some point, you may have to lay down the hammer to get employees focused and on point to hit hardcore deadlines. It won't be pretty, but sometimes you gotta do what you gotta do.
- *Politician*—Unfortunately, you've still got to manage up, and that's a completely different skill set than leading your employees. If you want to get ahead and be promoted, you need to figure out the complex dance of keeping your boss in the loop without overwhelming him or her, ensuring your boss is informed before problems rise to his or her level (preferably ideally, they never get there, but thinking that will never happen is a pipedream, not reality), and providing support to help get his or her projects completed on time and within budget.
- *Air traffic controller*—At any one point during a typical day, you're likely to have several major projects requiring your attention while you're also juggling a dozen or so smaller tasks—and those are only the items on your own to-do list. At the same time, you're also responsible for making sure that your direct reports do their jobs well and on time. An air traffic controller at Chicago's O'Hare airport could take scheduling lessons from today's manager (over a working lunch, of course).

Wearing so many hats can be stressful and exhausting. So why do it? Why push so hard to be a great manager? Because it can be one of the most magical experiences of your career. I've yet to find anything as exciting and rewarding as helping an employee blossom and surpass even her or his own expectations. It's truly a *magical* experience that has far eclipsed anything that I've ever done, including launching the Oxygen channel and founding InterActiveCorp. The legacy I'm proudest of are the people who have worked for me and then, through my guidance and encouragement, have gone on to do even more amazing things. They're the reason why I love managing people and what I think of on the days when I'm asking myself, "What have I gotten myself into?"

When you're feeling flustered, always remind yourself that you're smart and that you *can* figure this out. If you commit to being the best manager you can be and work hard to make that happen for each of your employees, you will succeed.

FOCUSING ON YOU

Unfortunately, many companies don't offer support for individual contributors who are making the transition to managers, or help veteran managers make adjustments needed to motivate and engage the four generations in the office today. In many organizations, managers are expected to figure all this stuff out on their own. Even someone who's been an outstanding manager for many years will need to make adjustments to maintain that same level of excellence in the new workplace reality.

So as you work to develop your employees' professional development plans, don't forget to pay attention to yourself, too! Commit *right now* to spending time focusing on what *you* need to keep your skills current in today's workplace. Don't wait for your boss to figure this out for you; instead, make it a priority and figure it out yourself. Here's what you can do to keep growing and learning in your current managerial position:

- *Participate in offsite training at least twice a year.* As difficult as it is to step out of the office for a while, it's important to get away from your day-to-day routines—and your desk—occasionally so you can both get a new perspective and focus on what you're learning. Online training programs don't count: this has to be a setting in which phones are turned off, there are no interruptions, and everyone is paying attention. Taking this time for your own professional development will make you a better manager back in the office.
- *Learn to be an effective communicator.* Your future success depends on your ability to communicate—managing up, down, and sideways all require superior communication skills. Communicating with people of different generations can be tricky because of variations in knowledge, experience, work ethic, and expectations. But if you keep in mind that all employees—even people within the same generation—are individuals, you can shove assumptions to the side and just ask each person what he or she wants. Strive to be a great communicator who actually listens to what employees say and is as transparent as possible with them. This approach can help you bridge differences and mitigate conflicts between generations and come up with solutions that motivate *all* your employees. If you focus on only one skill for yourself, make it this one.
- *Make developing talent a priority.* Ensuring that your employees' skills continue to improve not only motivates them, it also helps you in the long run. To move up, you need a successor—someone to do your current job while you assume greater responsibilities (or take on an entirely different role). So make it a priority to develop talent through formal planning in conjunction with your employees. (If you keep the plan only in your head, your best employees are likely to ditch you for a manager who's willing and able to discuss their career growth with them.) If you don't know how

to create a formal plan, seek guidance from your company's HR department, ask other well-respected leaders how they do official development, or just review chapter 9. If you establish a reputation for creating talent in your wake, the brightest and best people will want to come work for you. Then when the time comes for you to move up, you can focus on your new responsibilities, knowing that your old department will be in good hands.

- *Hire smart people.* Unfortunately, many managers lack this vital skill and end up having to hold a bad employee's hand instead of focusing on larger strategic issues. Don't just hire smart people—hire people who are smarter than you. Jack Welch famously said, "If you're the smartest person in the room, you've got real problems."[2] Learn not to be intimidated by people who are smarter than you, because hiring them will only make you look more brilliant! And smart people bring with them great ideas that not only benefit the organization but can help you, too, as they take on more responsibilities (that would otherwise fall to you).

- *Don't be satisfied with the status quo—push yourself to expand your skill set.* If you're not learning, you're stagnating. So keep pushing yourself to learn new skills, both within your company and in your industry at large. For example, because it's critical to understand how the organization makes money, learn how your product is made (and priced) as well as how much your product sells for (and the corresponding profit). Don't stop there, though: find out what it takes to sell the product to your customers and what customer support is needed for both the short term and the long term. Just as you should send your employees to talk with other department heads to learn about their processes, do the same thing yourself and perhaps identify projects in their areas with which you can assist. Figure out how you can add value (rather than merely increasing your knowledge), and then prioritize their projects. By volunteering to help, you expand your exposure to other company executives (which can help with a possible promotion down the line) and also learn something new.

- *Build a reputation as someone who gets stuff done.* Be a creative problem solver and build your reputation as someone who adds value across the organization, not just in your department. If you're bogged down in details, take a project management class to help you get organized and focus on the big-picture items (not just the minor tasks that can eat up your entire day). People are usually either part of the problem or part of the solution. If you focus on the latter, the company leadership will recognize that promoting you is imperative to the organization's growth and success.

Another development option for you to consider (especially if your company offers it) is one-on-one coaching, which is probably one of the most worthwhile development tools out there (second only to a relationship with the right mentor—see the next section). Having someone with whom you can discuss specific problems and ideas can be fantastic for developing skills quickly. Coaching is also great if you're focused on advanced leadership skills that are often less about technical components and more about the personal (self-awareness, self-management, integrity, authenticity), relational (interpersonal skills, effective communication, ability to inspire and influence), and organizational (political savvy, diplomacy, organizational awareness, tolerance for change and uncertainty) competencies needed at the senior-most levels.

Even if you work with a coach, though, it's important to find mentors both within and outside the organization who can help with your personal development. Each type has a different perspective: I found someone inside the company who helped me navigate the nuances of politics and personalities for example, and a mentor outside the company exposed me to a wider array of options for tackling problems and expanding my skills. Finding a mentor isn't just a matter of walking up to someone and asking him or her to be your mentor. It takes a lot of careful thought and work.

FINDING A MENTOR

If your company has a formal mentorship program, definitely apply for it, because companies often select the employees that they want to stick around (and, eventually, promote). If you aren't picked, don't fret—but ask follow-up questions to find out what you need to do in order to be selected in the next round. Check in periodically with your boss or HR to ensure you're actually making improvements needed to make you a stronger candidate for the program.

If your company doesn't have a formal program, don't let that stop you from finding a mentor. *Don't* just pick anyone, though! Do your homework to find the right fit.

Determine What You Hope to Achieve

When trying to identify who will be a good mentor, *start with the end in mind.* Figure out what you want to gain from a mentor and how he or she can help you reach your goals. Understanding what you hope to achieve in the relationship will help you narrow down which candidates to approach. At the same time, ask yourself what you can offer to a mentor that will make the relationship worthwhile for her. Remember, mentoring is a two-way street. In order to entice someone to mentor you (especially someone you don't know), you need a clear understanding of what you can bring to the table.

Know what you want before approaching anyone about establishing a mentoring relationship. Pinpointing in advance what's important to you will save time and hassle—for both you and your potential mentors.

Search for a Mentor

Review the list of managers in your company and identify one or two leaders who you know firsthand are highly respected by the employees. If you're new to the organization or there are managers whose leadership styles you're not quite sure about, chat with their direct reports. Most employees are delighted to talk about their bosses (and if they can't offer any suggestions or guidance, that is an interesting data point—though you should check with other sources to make sure you're getting a full picture).

If you prefer to have a mentor outside your company (or if there aren't any leaders in your organization whom you admire), review your own network for potential mentors. Possibilities include executives within your company, connections via LinkedIn, alumni from your alma mater, or people you know through other industry sources or group affiliations. Networking events, conferences, and trade shows can also be great venues for finding potential mentors.

Make the Initial Contact

After identifying a potential mentor, learn as much as you can about him or her before you reach out. See if you have any common connections on LinkedIn because, if you don't know a potential mentor personally, an introduction from an acquaintance you have in common can help you establish a connection (and perhaps help you make a favorable first impression, too).

If you're blindly reaching out to someone with whom you have no connections, go for a quick e-mail introduction that mentions common ground, specific interests or discussion points, and asks for a brief, 15-minute phone conversation or in-person meeting. Hopefully, this brief connection with your potential mentor will pique his or her curiosity enough to communicate further with you. Being specific about what you seek from a mentor will help that person determine whether the two of you are a good mentor match. And be clear and succinct in your note: if you ramble in this e-mail, your potential mentor may assume that you ramble on the phone and in person, too.

If you don't hear from your potential mentor soon, follow up but don't hound him or her. If a check-in two to three weeks after your initial contact bears no fruit, you should assume that he or she isn't interested in mentoring you right now. You can still try to maintain a relationship (even if it's one way), however, by passing along articles or news that may interest that person.

Make a Good Impression

Always keep in mind that your mentor is doing you a favor (this goes for internal programs as well), so make sure that you are appreciative of the time he or she takes out of his or her schedule to assist you. I strongly recommend traveling to your mentor's location in order to maximize your time together. You want to make it as easy as possible for your mentor to help you!

During your first meeting or phone call, ask for advice on a single topic or problem. Don't overwhelm your mentor with every question you ever wanted to answer! Instead, use this opportunity to build rapport with a future mentor.

The goal is to establish a relationship for the long term—not have a comprehensive one-and-done meeting. It's definitely okay to discuss goals for the length of your mentoring relationship, but again, keep in mind that if this is a new connection, you don't want to overwhelm your mentor to the point of thinking that this relationship is more than he or she has time for.

Also, don't make assumptions about your mentor's time or preferred modes of interaction. Ask your mentor how he or she would like to communicate and how often, and if you settle on a time limit (15 or 30 minutes, for example), be respectful of it—and your mentor's time—and don't go beyond it.

Getting the Most out of Mentoring

The advice you get may not always be easy to swallow, but keep in mind that your mentor is successful for a reason and probably knows what he or she is talking about. Here are a few more helpful tips for working with a mentor:

- *Set pride aside.* Resolve to be both teachable and coachable.
- *Cultivate the relationship.* Ask questions and listen actively to the answers.
- *Help your mentor help you.* If you have a specific question or need, let your mentor know. It's up to you to do the homework for your meetings and set the schedule.
- *Return the favor.* You're bound to excel at some skill that can benefit your mentor. Mentorship is a two-way street, so try to help your mentor in any way that you can.
- *Have fun!* Although your ultimate goal is to learn, nothing says you can't enjoy the time you spend with your mentor. Make your meetings a time you both look forward to.

Remember, you and your mentor both get out of this relationship what you put into it, so work hard to make it worth everyone's time. If nurtured carefully, the relationship you have with your mentor can be one that lasts throughout your career!

MOVING FROM TACTICAL DOER TO STRATEGIC THINKER

Once you shift from being an individual contributor to managing others, you'll need to be able to focus on larger strategic issues for the department as a whole. After all, you have to provide oversight to your direct reports, and that means focusing on the bigger picture—and not only on your tasks. The need to focus on more strategic issues will only increase as you continue to move up within your organization. That can be challenging to do, because every employee's inclination is to deal with what's right in front of him or her—that is, what's due today. And yes, sometimes you do have to take that "here and now" approach. But if you find hours or even days going by during which you're focused only on short-term tactical issues, you're doing yourself, your position, and your company a disservice. As you move up the ranks, your job is to pay more attention to the strategic concerns that inform your organization's long-term goals. Here are four steps for moving from the tactical to the strategic.

Step 1: Delegate the Small Stuff

It's hard to let go of a task, especially when it's something quick that you're sure you can knock out in 20 minutes. The next thing you know, though, that one small task has turned into three tasks—and you've just killed an hour. Also, rarely does anything truly take "only a few minutes," especially with the constant interruptions caused by e-mail, texts, and phone calls.

So delegate as much of the small stuff as you can *right now*. If you can't delegate a small task, ask yourself whether it's really essential. Remember, 20 percent of your efforts results in 80 percent of the profits, so make sure you focus only on stuff that *matters* (and avoid falling into the trap of doing a task simply because it's easy).[3] And recognize that even though it's not always an easy thing to do, sometimes you have to say no to the nonessential stuff so you can focus on what's important.

Step 2: Block Time for Strategizing

Spend time each day plotting out what you're going to accomplish that day. (I typically spend the first 30 minutes of my day doing this.) On that list put the tactical items that definitely must get done (for me, these include client-related tasks), but be very strict about how you define the "musts." If you don't, the tactical tasks can take over your day! Right after you finish building your action item list, either jump right into strategy mode or block time for this exercise later that day. I make time for strategizing every single day, even if I can devote only half an hour to it. This daily habit is a key part of my professional life—and it should be part of yours, too!

Step 3: Evaluate Strategic Issues

What exactly does it mean to *strategize*? Strategizing means evaluating your long-term plans and goals and answering these two questions:

1. Do your plans align with the future you see for yourself professionally? (For me, as an entrepreneur, that means asking myself if I'm moving toward securing future business that is meaningful to me.)
2. Do you spend time each week working toward your company's strategic objectives? (When I worked at Oxygen Media, answering this question meant evaluating my department's goals and determining if they were in line with the organization's long-term vision.)

If you answer no to either of these questions, you need to reconsider how you're spending your time. Reprioritize your time by dumping the "nice to have" items and focusing on the "must haves" to reach your strategic objectives.

Step 4: Make a Plan

After determining *what* to focus on, it's time to figure out *how* to make your plan happen. To do that, prioritize your strategic objectives and set *real deadlines* for them. Unless you choose dates that matter, you might not feel genuine pressure to work on your plan—and your strategic goals will remain mere pipe dreams. With end dates in mind, map out how many hours a week it will take to accomplish these objectives. Then block out on your calendar the time you'll need to work toward them. Every bit of time helps, and you'll be amazed at what you can get accomplished: spending just 1 hour each weekday on this work, for example, yields 20 hours a month of concentrated effort.

From the moment you're promoted to your first managerial position, it's time to focus on strategic issues, not just on the day-to-day tasks that need to be accomplished. By spending part of your day in this pursuit, you're preparing yourself to continue to move up the corporate ladder, because the more senior you are, the more the focus of your day should be on strategic issues. Set the stage now for your continued success!

NOTES

1. Emerson, Ralph Waldo. "Essay VIII: Heroism." 1841. http://www.emerson central.com/heroism.htm.
2. Mimaroglu, Alp. "The Magic of Leadership: Observations from 10 of the Most Successful People in Business." *Entrepreneur* online. April 26, 2016. http://www.entrepreneur.com/slideshow/274280.
3. The idea that 80% of the results stem from 20% of the causes is known as the Pareto Principle and was named by Joseph M. Juran. For more information, see http://www.juran.com/about-us/legacy/.

CASE STUDY - CHEGG

Website: www.chegg.com
Location: Santa Clara, California
Total employees: 361 US full-time employees, 324 globally
Employee demographics: 60 percent Millennials, 40 percent non-Millennials
What it does: Chegg, the Student Hub, offers 24/7 online tutoring, test prep, textbook rentals, and other educational services for high school and college students
Interviewee: Dan Rosensweig—Chairman, Chief Executive Officer, President

BACKGROUND

Based in Silicon Valley, Chegg has tested numerous strategies both to retain employees and to improve the working relationship between generations. Rosensweig refers to Silicon Valley as "the canary in the coal mine" when it comes to companies having to think about a multigenerational workforce and being on the cutting edge of providing corporate perks. He describes the region as a very expensive suburb with little nightlife or culture—which is why younger employees, particularly those without families, choose to live in nearby, vibrant San Francisco.

The company's history of diversity in other areas has allowed it to be vigilant about generational differences. There's a good mix of employees born in the United States and abroad, 44 percent of the staff is female, and its approach toward ethnic diversity is also broadening. Rosensweig explains, "We are trying to be more representative, because the students that we serve are more representative of America versus what corporate America generally looked like. So it's been in our best interest."

Chegg developed its programs both by listening to employees and by examining behavior. When the company's annual satisfaction survey revealed that a large percentage of the staff had student loans and HR noted that not many Millennials were signing up for the 401(k) program, for example, the company conceptualized ways of helping employees with their financial aid debt. Recruiters noted that many job candidates asked if working out of the Santa Clara office was necessary, which prompted management to rethink both its policies and its office space. "We brainstormed with our benefits people," says Rosensweig. "We said, 'What kind of things do we do that can support the lifestyles that these folks want to live?'"

BENEFITS

Recognizing that each generation had its own individual needs and desires, Chegg reworked its benefits packages. For example, in addition to the traditional 401(k) program that has been offered for years, Chegg offers to match an employee's student loan payments, because Millennials prefer to get rid of debt rather than accumulate savings. The 401(k) program, however, is still offered, as the senior employees still expect it.

Having a variety of medical programs has also proven popular. "We even offer pet insurance," says Rosensweig, because the younger portion of the workforce doesn't have kids but many do have pets. For the older slice of employees, Chegg offers options such as emergency caregivers for those with kids or even older parents.

Flexible work schedules—both for Millennials who expect it and for older employees who need to, say, pick up their kids after school—have also been introduced to make working at Chegg more appealing to both prospective and current staff. Many employees jump back on their computers at home once they've finished shuttling the kids around. And because the company has proven loyal to its employees, the employees have reciprocated by not taking advantage of such flexibility. "We just care about the productivity," said Rosensweig, who is quite happy with how productive his employees remain while still being able to balance their personal lives.

COMPANY CULTURE

Rosensweig relates a story of how he asked a summer intern where she was going when he spotted her leaving the office at 2:30 in the afternoon. She answered that she was headed to Starbucks to finish up her work because she found the office too distracting. Her response was a revelation to him in how much has changed with how and where today's employees (of all ages) prefer to work.

Now that technology allows for remote working, even the older generations have availed themselves of the conveniences. "If I can FaceTime my daughter in Copenhagen every day," says Rosensweig, "why can't I FaceTime an employee if I need them?" And that's exactly what Chegg employees have begun doing, allowing everyone on staff a more flexible work routine that appeals to all ages and takes advantage of new innovations. "Not everybody's going to behave the same way," admits Rosensweig, "and as management, you try not to expect them to. We like to say that we have multiple cultures but one set of values, and if we all live by the same values, then it's okay to have multiple [working] cultures and work styles."

Scheduling plays a big role in work style. Chegg management noted that even though employees with families didn't want to take part in after-work bonding activities, the younger staffers showed more interest in doing so. The annual company picnic is no longer planned for a weekend, Rosensweig says, because although when he first entered the workforce he was obligated to attend such company events, "this generation doesn't think that way." Older generations have changed their personal lifestyles as well; family obligations often make weekend events impossible. So while Millennials were the ones who prompted management to give more thought as to when the annual event was held, the move to during work hours appealed to everyone.

"We try to balance things," says Rosensweig. "What can we do during the workday, and what can we schedule for after hours? We recognize that people of different generations have different responsibilities during and after work." Thus the company tries to mix up the timing of events so that everyone has the chance to participate in team-building activities. "We're just more cognizant of it [than we were before]," says Rosensweig, "and we try different things. Sometimes we succeed and sometimes we don't, but we generally get good karma credit for having tried."

Rosensweig also discusses the differences between the generations' company loyalty. "When I moved here from New York, where I was with my previous company for 15 years, I was stunned by the rate of turnover: the average employee stays 2.3 years at a company out here." He believes Silicon Valley's progressive, employee-friendly culture has contributed to this turnover, but that generational differences have as well. Younger employees are ready to jump-start the job search after only a couple of years, whereas the older generation stays far longer because of the need for security, desire to maintain benefits, and hope that company loyalty will pay off in terms of promotions.

Younger employees' capricious views toward job attachment make it harder for older employees to invest in somebody who may seek new opportunities in a relatively short amount of time. "That was never the way we older generations grew up," says Rosensweig, who also says this has probably been the biggest multi-generational challenge for Chegg. Managers just don't want to invest time in an employee only to find that they've trained for a competitor. The combined programs and policies that Chegg has implemented in the past few years have improved Millennial turnover rate by 40 percent.

PHYSICAL WORK ENVIRONMENT

After years of hearing job candidates bemoan the commute from San Francisco to Santa Clara, Chegg opened up a San Francisco office and began offering transportation (with air conditioning and Wi-Fi, of course) between the two locations. Company-provided bicycles in Santa Clara allow employees to easily get from the train station to the office.

Such changes in the physical work environment have appealed not only to Millennials but to the older workforce, who appreciate convenience and the occasional change in scenery just as much as their younger counterparts.

Employee Reviews

Millennials' desire for constant and immediate feedback prompted Chegg to ditch its old system of annual reviews. Rosensweig cites the oft-repeated belief that the younger generation wants to move up the corporate ladder as quickly as possible and expects to be vice president practically the day after graduation. Veteran employees resented what they saw as Millennials' sense of entitlement.

"If you create the right kind of values and culture and you set the expectations right, you eliminate those as issues," Rosensweig says. "If you don't set the expectations up front, it's not unreasonable for people who are making major contributions in their first year to wonder why they're not in the same meeting with somebody else."

Chegg achieved the goal of setting expectations and providing more frequent reviews through a system called Fast Feedback, which allows managers to communicate both the positive and the negative in a timely and effective manner. At the end of a project, Rosensweig says, a manager can tell an employee, "'You did a phenomenal job with this, or next time you address this, maybe we should think about doing it this way.' Fast Feedback has been extremely helpful in communication between the generations because it eliminates the mystery between them."

While Rosensweig didn't have exact numbers on the cost to implement Fast Feedback, he said that "the return was much greater than any financial cost" in that it satisfied employees in every sector of the age spectrum.

RECRUITING

Chegg continually reviews its offerings for younger employees to see what could entice them either to move closer to the Santa Clara office or to make the long commute from San Francisco. One idea was to offer events that appealed to that age group, such as cultural walks through the city and a summer intern "Olympics." Such activities, says Rosensweig, demonstrate Chegg's efforts to offer opportunities for forging new relationships to employees who don't yet "have families or children and who are looking to build bonds and connect to other people."

"We're in the education business," explains Rosensweig. "The college class of 2020 is sort of a really interesting watermark, because they were born the same year that Google was born. They've never known a day without the Internet, Netflix, or iPhones." That means that in order to attract their target employees—recent college graduates who best understand what students want—Chegg has to be forward-thinking and "create environments that are more in line with [Millennials'] modernized expectations." These expectations include the assumption that everything work related—from documents to HR forms—should be on demand, easy to use, customizable, and mobile accessible, thus making it easier for employees to choose when and where to get their work done.

Customization played a big role in one of the more popular perks common to Silicon Valley: the free lunch. Whereas Chegg used to offer one option to all employees—Mexican one day, Chinese the next—it now allows individuals to order from a variety of restaurants and different cuisines, each and every workday. This not only appeals to Millennials, who were the instigators behind the change, but also to employees with specialized dietary needs or desires, such as vegetarians, diabetics, or simply those who choose to eat healthy. "It's stuff like that," says Rosensweig, "that we would never have thought of just five years ago."

SUMMARY

By implementing new HR offerings and evolving the work culture, Chegg has decreased its turnover rate of Millennials by 40 percent in the past four years. All the new policies and programs have not only increased employee satisfaction but have also made a marked difference in intergenerational communication. "What we've seen is the older generation mentoring about how to be productive, what it means to meet deadlines, and how to be part of a team," says Rosensweig. "And the Millennials have helped us all learn how to be part of a team remotely." It also gives Millennials the constant acknowledgment they desire and the more senior employees a solid way to communicate and record that acknowledgment.

CASE STUDY - CONSULTANTS: LEADERSHIP DEVELOPMENT SERVICES, LLC, AND RGP

INTERVIEWEES

Bridget Graham—Senior Consultant, RGP (www.rgp.com)

Dr. Lois J. Zachary—President, Leadership Development Services, LLC (www.leadservs.com)

Consultants have the benefit of gaining insight into a wide variety of companies—how they work, what the culture is like, and how employees interact. And while companies come in all shapes and sizes, the similarities often outweigh the differences. One of those similarities is the clash of the generations, which occurs in nearly every industry, from health care to tech.

Although she's never been brought into a company specifically to address a multigenerational matter, Bridget Graham, a senior consultant at RGP, says that while most companies don't usually identify generational differences as the cause, "inevitably it comes up in many issues I'm handling."

Dr. Lois J. Zachary, president of Leadership Development Services, notes that there is definitely a difference in the generations' mind-sets, approaches, and ways of working. Her company, which promotes mentoring as a tool for leadership competency, finds mentoring to be key in bridging those divides. "Mentoring is something both Gen Xers and Millennials crave," she explains. "It's a way to feel connected, to feel like somebody cares about you, and to feel supported."

The following are areas where the generational clash most often arises, and what you can do to overcome them in the workplace.

LEADERSHIP

"To be a leader, you have to be a mentor," says Zachary, who views mentoring as a leadership competency. "It's part of your growth and part of what you do as a leader."

With the increase in the number of younger employees managing their older colleagues, the concept of just who's leading whom can get fuzzy. Graham likes to remind junior managers that just because someone doesn't have a higher title doesn't mean he or she is not a leader. "A leader is someone who steers the group," she explains. For example, a department might have one employee who is more vocal than the others, thus influencing the group's attitude and behavior as a whole. "You want that perceived leader to be an ally," she stresses. "You want their buy-in. They need to feel included, respected."

If that perceived leader is a veteran employee who isn't on board with the manager's direction, a different tactic might be needed to win him or her over so that the rest of the team falls in line. "You'll have the least amount of resistance if you have that perceived leader as your ally," Graham says. "Take those older workers on a journey. Make them feel like they're already part of the process, rather than simply being given orders."

When it comes to older workers managing younger ones, Graham reminds the more seasoned workers of the similarities between the generations. "I explain that what's important to you could be important to them, but how you arrive at it is different." She uses core math as an example, pointing out that although the younger generations have learned how to multiply and divide using a completely different technique than what was once taught in schools, we all still arrive at the same answer: "It's just the method we use that's completely different."

Teams will work toward a common goal, but they might take different approaches to reach it. A Millennial's desire to complete a task at a café doesn't mean she or he isn't working toward the group goal, while a Gen Xer's late work hours needn't be adhered to by other employees.

However, there are some environments in which consistent processes need to be followed. Graham relates how, while assisting with an issue within a health-care environment, she encountered a young health-care provider who wasn't following procedure. "In a health-care setting, there is no gray," Grahams explains. "Vitals have to be taken a certain way, stats have to be written in a particular manner. There's a reason why these are done a certain way, and it's critical to the way a health-care service runs." But the veteran health-care provider helping to orient the young recruit noticed that her charge wasn't following these protocols, and she reminded her on numerous occasions to do so.

Graham isn't sure whether the younger provider was being stubborn, thinking her way was better, or simply couldn't grasp the correct method, but after numerous violations, the facility let her go. "She was qualified," says Graham, but "she just wouldn't—or couldn't—follow the protocol." If a company has an absolute standard that must be followed (with serious consequences when it's not), then do it. But if there is wiggle room, what's the harm in allowing it to allow for individualism?

Zachary has found mentoring to be one of the best ways to improve leadership. These days, she says, the new trend in mentoring programs is to see it as a partnership, rather than as a top-down model. In this way, both mentors and mentees gain more equally. As an example, she mentions Boomers or employees who have been with a company for a long time and who often continue doing what they've always done since they started their careers. "By mentoring somebody of a different generation, their perspectives get transformed," Zachary explains. "They see things through different eyes, and they're able to continue to grow and develop."

Mentoring programs are not one size fits all, Zachary says, and describes how she gets to know a company's culture before suggesting what might work for it. In addition to interviewing employees to gain a better understanding of their personalities, wants, and needs, Zachary maps out clearly defined goals: "You have to create value and visibility for mentoring. You have to have the right training. You have to offer multiple mentoring opportunities, especially for different generations." To ensure the program is a success, she encourages companies to have safety nets, such as providing the time for employees to participate and establishing mentoring coaches to help both mentors and mentees, should problems arise.

Reward and recognition are basic components of any successful mentoring program (and right in line with Millennials' desires). While some companies offer monetary rewards, for others mentoring is just a normal part of running a business. Either way, making that show of appreciation, both throughout the process and once a mentorship has come to an end, should be built into the program. "It's really a celebration of learning, a celebration of growth, a celebration of development," she says.

Mentoring can also help build better employee relationships. Zachary stresses the importance of employees making an effort to get to know each other, which can help break down the stereotypes and misconceptions that often thwart productivity. As an example, she notes that some mentoring programs have Boomers serving as mentees to younger generations, which often makes the more seasoned employees skeptical at first, believing that there's nothing to learn from younger colleagues. But once the program is under way, those doubts are often eradicated.

"I tell my older workers not to listen to the stereotypes," Graham says, echoing Zachary. "Within that selection of younger workers is a variety of different people, who come from different cultures and socioeconomic backgrounds that have influenced their individual work ethics. Understand who they are as people, not as a collective whole." Getting to know each other enables employees to better understand how to work together and even leverage their best assets.

FLEXIBILITY

According to the consultants, nearly every generation shows some aversion to change, just in different ways. Older generations worry that they won't be able to learn a new technology, while the younger generations often feel the improvement isn't good enough (and more should be done).

As with the case of the health-care provider mentioned earlier, Millennials tend to be as stuck in their ways as their older peers. "I've noticed it in every industry—financial, health-care, tech, you name it," says Graham. "When they come in fresh out of school, they feel as though everything is antiquated. 'Why aren't we on board with the new way of doing things?'" She's noticed the trend becoming more prevalent over the last several years.

This Millennial mind-set can compound a situation already made difficult by the older generation's aversion to change, especially when it comes to technology. Graham mentions a situation in which a financial institution was looking to introduce new software that the older workers opposed simply because they were comfortable with the old way. Adding to the voice of dissatisfaction were the Millennials, who thought the new software didn't resolve enough of the problems inherent to the old system. Even though the younger generation offered solutions, not all of them were practical or even possible. No one felt that his or her needs were being met.

In the end, management had to step in and issue the final verdict: the change was coming, whether everyone liked it or not. Once employees realized that the introduction of the new software was inevitable, the protesting ceased. "Eventually, everyone adapts," says Graham, which is why companies shouldn't allow employee resistance, at any level, to hinder innovation and their evolution.

WORK ETHIC AND STYLE

Both Graham and Zachary find work ethic to be one of the areas that exhibits the biggest difference between the generations. Graham sees the more senior generation as committed to the company, the middle generation as committed to the people at the company, and the younger generations more interested in how they can advance their careers and in what's in it for them. "For the younger workers, it has to make sense to them," says Graham. "It has to have meaning for them. On the other hand, Gen Xers are torn between wanting to be with their families and feeling they should be at work, and they choose one or the other, depending on the situation."

Whatever work ethic the company promotes, it has to be consistent so as not to show favoritism to any one group. Graham mentions a situation in which a Millennial called in sick several days in a row, but a coworker noticed her posting photos of herself on social media while on a beach overseas. The company had a difficult decision to make, and Graham advised terminating the employee for her dishonesty, citing how keeping her would impact morale. "She did this so boldly, so in your face," Graham says. When the company opted not to fire or even discipline the employee, against Graham's advice, there was indeed discontent, particularly among the older workers, who felt that the company showed too much leniency to an employee who showed such lack of respect and work ethic.

Because they're the newest to enter the workforce, Millennials tend to get the brunt of the criticism. In addition to being seen as flouting authority, the younger generation is often described by older generations as desiring continuous acknowledgment. But even those raised during the "everyone gets a trophy" era are as hardworking as their older counterparts. They just have different motivations.

Managers should see this as a plus. Motivation and acknowledgment, after all, come with very small price tags—in fact, they're free. No matter how the workforce may have been when you landed your first job, the world has changed, and it doesn't take much to acknowledge a contribution—for team members of every generation. (Remember: Be consistent.) With Millennials in particular, acknowledgment can help bridge generation gap, further earning their trust and cementing their loyalty to the team. Even the older generations wouldn't begrudge a pat on the back for a job well done.

BENEFITS

Companies that have identified what the next generations want and make that part of the compensation package are better poised to recruit the cream of the crop. That's one reason Millennials and the first wave of Generation Z are flocking toward start-ups, says Graham. "Most startup C-suites are composed wholly of the younger generation, so they already know what attracts those candidates—and they're giving it to them."

The Internet has made it easier than ever for people to compare offerings, while social media has provided even deeper insight into the everyday lives of our friends and family, including their places of work. Because of this, nearly everyone knows about the over-the-top benefits that have become the norm in Silicon Valley. Google's never-ending smorgasbord of snacks and gourmet meals is legendary, while Apple throws beer bashes with live entertainment from some of the biggest bands in the music biz, in addition to offering more practical perks, such as free shuttle service and stipends for commuters. Widespread knowledge of these benefits—across the generations—means that companies have to get competitive to attract talent.

While there's been a trend toward corporate behemoths cutting back on some of the more extravagant and unnecessary perks, it's a buyer's market when it comes to job hunting, even with the sluggish economy. Prospective employees still hold the power, and the rising wave of Millennials will hold out for exactly what they want, whether that be more paid time off, a flexible health-care plan, or simply an environment in which they are assured acknowledgment for a job well done. They can afford to be picky, not only because of the offerings, but because, unlike their older counterparts, they're more likely to move back in with Mom and Dad while they continue their job search.

Funny enough, says Graham, even though Millennials are vocal about wanting the sky when it comes to benefits, they don't always take advantage of them. "They care about benefits, but only in that they want to make sure they're getting everything they can," she explains. "They want to feel they are working at a company with that robust package, because that makes Company A better than Company B." Even if they don't sign up for the improved offerings, just having the choice makes Millennials—and other generations—happier. "They feel good knowing how many options they have."

CASE STUDY - ELECTRONIC ARTS

Website: www.ea.com

Location: Based in Redwood City, California, with 31 global locations around the world

Founded: 1982, public company

Total employees: 8,400; 40 percent within the United States, 60 percent outside the United States

Employee demographics: 50 percent Millennials, with the rest being a mix of Gen X and Baby Boomers

What it does: Develops video games

Interviewee: Gabrielle Toledano—Executive Vice President and Chief Talent Officer, overseeing HR, Real Estate and Facilities, and Corporate Social Responsibility

BACKGROUND

In some industries, employee age can play a crucial role in the business, such as when it's important to have an affinity with the customer's interests. Video game pioneer Electronic Arts understands this well, because its players (EA's term for its customers) range in age from up-and-coming Generation Zers to Boomers. The company's workforce reflects that demographic: half of the employee base is made up on Millennials, with most of the remaining employees comprising Gen X and Baby Boomer employees.

"We have to have a generationally diverse workforce, because our employees make the games that appeal to these different audiences," says Toledano, who has been with the company for more than a decade. She adds, "We have a huge diversity of roles at EA" to reflect the diversity of EA's players. Because generational knowledge is so critical to the company's success, EA has spent a great deal of time (and money) figuring out what's important to employees at each stage of their lives and uses that information to better manage its workforce: "We've identified the behaviors and values we need to exhibit for employees of all ages, and then we created programs and a culture at EA that enable us to lead more effectively given this information."

With more than 25 years in human resources, the HR veteran has noticed how workplaces, particularly those of younger companies or in more progressive fields, have become less hierarchical and more team based, with a focus on community to encourage camaraderie. There's also a shift in what's deemed acceptable in the office. "A few years ago, you'd restrict people from accessing external websites. Browsing the Internet on the job was a red flag," she observes. But that has changed, particularly at EA, where staying up to date with innovations and fostering creative thinking, including through online social interactions, is the cornerstone of the business. Toledano admits that EA may be an extreme in these areas, in terms of its leniency: "We're a video game company based in California, so our mind-set is different. Employees are playing video games, surfing the web, doing whatever they want. We're in tech and entertainment, so you have to be inclusive and open-minded if you want to be a modern business and not restrict your talent pool. You have to be able to evolve." This mind-set allows for a more creative employee community and work environment.

COMPANY CULTURE

When asked about the corporate culture, Toledano mentions the importance of transparency—and how Millennials have played a large role in increasing the practice within the company. The cohort's desire for openness and accountability has resulted in sweeping changes in many areas. One is the company's approach to mentoring.

Understanding younger consumers' expectations is critical to the company's future. "We used to sell discs only to retailers," explains Toledano, "but now we also sell direct to consumers digitally. We needed a workforce of digital natives, which is what Millennials are. Almost everything has been digital their whole lives. That prompted us to create intergenerational communities that we call guilds." Unlike the traditional system of mentoring, which has seasoned employees guiding the newer hires, EA's guilds spread across functional areas, including software engineering, production, design, and analytics. These guilds foster cross-generational idea sharing, as well as a better understanding of generation-based and work styles based on your generation. The result has been a more closely knit workforce who communicate easily and—even better—a surge in ideas, many of which have made it into the video games that EA produces.

CAREER DEVELOPMENT

Toledano states that career development ranks at the top of employees' wishes—and Millennials are voicing this desire with passion and clarity. "They seem to want more feedback than other generations do," she says. "They want to make sure there's another opportunity following the current one, to ensure their mobility. There's none of the old-school custom of waiting until you're tapped on the shoulder. Employees, in particular Millennials, really want to know how the company plans to help them progress."

That has made EA reexamine its approach to employee development, the result of which is a more transparent system that clearly and succinctly details the skills, competencies, and experience an employee needs to move up a level on the ladder. There is no guessing—it's very clear what's needed to move from software engineer level 1 to software engineer level 2, for example (each level and position have very specific requirements that an employee needs to meet before he or she is considered for a promotion). The *how* also matters, though—an employee may have the capabilities and experience to get promoted, but it also matters how well he or she works with others and how he or she gets the job done. The employee's supervisor makes the determination on the soft skills (the how) and if he or she is indeed ready to be promoted. Toledano describes this further: "You can't just have the *what*, so your teamwork, your values, all that matters when getting a job done." When asked how they accomplished this, she responds, "We've done a ton of job-leveling work to describe transparently how you can get from one level to the other." This effort is the culmination of years for work and is subject to constant evolution and updating.

Toledano has always made it a point to have at least biweekly one-on-ones with her direct reports but acknowledges that not all managers provide such frequent dialogue and feedback, which is something Millennials need. This desire for more frequent check-ins led to the abolition of the annual review process and forced ranking that is de facto in many more traditional companies. Instead, EA's current methodology provides quarterly reviews (without a rating scale attached). To help guide managers on what to do during these sessions, they are provided questions to ask their employees (although they can add to the list as well, of course). The conversations are more coaching in nature, stressing opportunities and development areas. The guidelines and questions make the process both more transparent and consistent among employees. The resulting Managing for Results program, built in house, provides a laser focus on career development and coaching, as well as 360-degree feedback from peers and other hierarchical levels. Combined, this data makes for more constructive and developmentally focused conversations.

While Toledano acknowledges that some of these changes arose to appease Millennials, the whole process of performance management was in need of an overhaul and many companies are heading toward more frequent check-ins anyway. Regular, consistent feedback, she says, "is just basic good management" and more useful in the long run to develop employees. And while some managers feel that the new system requires more time commitment, it also has led to more engaged employees and higher performance. It has forced managers to rethink their management styles and spend time on their employees' career development, which formerly took a back seat to their other managerial responsibilities. To help employees learn the new system and methodology, EA rolled out "a lot of online training for managers to educate them on the importance of more frequent check-ins with their employees."

With these changes in career development in mind, EA retired its old performance management system, which Toledano says was driven by the goal of documenting problems for legal purposes. "None of that documentation helped anyone legally," she says. "In fact, it hurt us, because most managers don't write down negative performance issues." She says that some managers would even give higher ratings than warranted by an employee's performance, then turn around and want to fire the employee: "The old previous system of measuring performance was broken."

And that broken system caused problems for Toledano, who would have to explain to an employee why a bonus didn't match his or her rating. She knew a huge revamp was in order, and when trying to decide just how to implement it, she reflected back on her time at Microsoft, where Bill Gates adamantly opposed the forced distribution rating system, seeing it as an artificial assessment of true performance that squeezed people into predefined boxes. "Bill's was a good side to be on," she says, looking back. "You can't be boxed into something that's arbitrary, not fact based. It was never a good practice to explain to someone that his or her rating was low just because he or she was new. That was not motivating top performers."

The transparency that Millennials desire has also affected how salaries are communicated. If employees want to know how they compare to their peers, management can provide a breakdown (taking privacy into consideration, of course). For example, if a software engineer wants to know how he or she ranks in pay, managers often provide a spreadsheet of other salaries at his or her level, with the names suppressed. As an unexpected benefit, this policy falls right in line with 2016's California Fair Pay Act, which aims to close the gender-pay gap by requiring employers to be transparent about how much employees who performed "substantially similar" work earn. Toledano predicts that such laws will become nationwide in time: "I'm all for that, too!"

Under the merit-based Managing for Results system, there hasn't been a single problem with distributing bonuses without ratings, and the conversation now focuses on an employee's quarterly performance and where her or his career is headed. "Employees want to know what's going well and what they can do better so that they can be successful," says Toledano. And the new system is working not only for Millennials but also for Gen Xers, who make up a majority of the managers giving the reviews. "Their employee engagement is going up, they're getting good feedback, they're retaining their employees—they're happy," she adds.

Another change in the company environment was the elimination of the term *poaching*, which refers to one department stealing an employee from another. Poaching used to be forbidden at most companies, but at EA that policy has since changed in favor of allowing employees to have more mobility. "We need to show these opportunities to our employees," Toledano says, returning to the idea of transparency. "There's no such thing as poaching, as far as I'm concerned." Today, EA has an internal job posting system as robust as its external one, and employees can apply for any position they like. The company expects managers to create robust and engaging roles for their teams. If employees are high potential and not engaged, EA benefits when a manager from another team can recruit them into his or her team and keep them within the company.

Toledano offers managers this advice on transparency: don't make a one-off decision that sets a precedent that can't be justified by the context of the situation. Don't support something that you wouldn't be able to justify if the decision got out to the whole company: "I've encouraged my teams to have a fairness filter. That's a personal value of mine."

RECRUITING

Millennials have proven to be quite different from their Gen X predecessors when it comes to hiring. "We've had to create a new and distinct method for onboarding our Millennial college grads in ways that we don't have to onboard Gen Xers," Toledano says.

Freshly minted graduates crave community, and EA has created precisely that, which it is developing to apply to all new hires: "Whereas in the old onboarding system, a new college graduates would show up for their first day and pretty much be on their own, we've created an onboarding experience and connected them with a peer community that carries them through their entire career here." So on their first day, all the new graduate hires form a cohort, and it's emphasized (and reinforced) that they are a team, even once they go to their separate departments. That team (along with their managers and department coworkers) is a resource to help new employees as they adjust to work life at EA.

SUMMARY

Although Millennials have inspired many of the changes made at EA, the benefits have been felt across all generations. The workplace landscape is changing across all industries, but being the vanguard of these transformations has allowed the company—which has long been known as a pioneer—to remain a choice employer in its field.

CASE STUDY - HY-KO PRODUCTS

Website: www.hy-ko.com
Location: Northfield, Ohio
Founded: 1949
Total employees: 204; 30 percent are salaried, 70 percent are hourly, 0.02 percent are located outside the United States
Employee demographics: 41 percent Traditionalists and Boomers, 34 percent Generation Xers, 25 percent Millennials
What it does: Manufactures consumer goods such as numbers and letters for signs, as well as keys and key accessories
Interviewee: Alice Bissett—Vice President, Human Resources

BACKGROUND

Hy-Ko has been a family-run business since its inception. "The culture is slowly changing from a mom-and-pop vibe to more of a corporate feel," Bissett shares. "We're being more consistent in how we administer policies, which not everyone appreciates. It's been a challenge to keep long-term employees motivated as they watch the company evolve," which it has done partly to appeal to younger recruits—and to stay competitive as an employer for all ages.

As an established company, Hy-Ko has a current employee base consisting mainly of the upper end of the generations, although recent recruiting efforts are beginning to draw in younger cohorts. While the company has a healthy environment that sees little conflict between the generations, Bissett did notice areas that could be improved when she started with the company in 2014.

Issues such as younger employees frequently calling in sick (due to the company's harsh time-off policy) and difficulty in hiring Millennials (due to the company's benefits package) were identified. Bissett sought to tackle them one at time. "We're trying to make it a better, happier place to be," she says. Another part of the challenge confronting the HR vice president was simply enacting and change, because "it's really hard to change thinking in a company that's mature." But change it she did.

BENEFITS AND RECRUITMENT

When Bissett arrived at Hy-Ko, paid time off (PTO) was not one of the company's more stellar offerings, particularly for new hires: employees did not receive any vacation time off until after they were employed with the company one full year. This was especially difficult for employees in the plant, because they were penalized with points for taking time off; when they had too many points, they were terminated. "They'd call in sick because they didn't have vacation days, and then they'd get a point for that," says Bissett. "Before you knew it, they reached the limit where our policy dictated we had to let them go. We have to treat everybody the same, so we couldn't keep one employee who had 'pointed out' and let another one go. We were losing really good employees who, through no fault of their own, didn't have the time off they needed."

Because vacation had to be accrued, new employees started off with no vacation time at all their first year. PTO also did not roll over to the following year, which resulted in a lot more absences among younger employees, who made it a point to use all their days. At the other end of the spectrum were disgruntled older employees who, unable to find a convenient time to be away from the office, wound up forfeiting their vacation days. To motivate employees to come to work, the company offered month-end events such as pizza parties and ice cream socials. Those helped, but the problem still persisted.

At the same time, Bissett noticed that potential new recruits to the company were negotiating PTO more than any other benefit as they went through the recruitment process, and prospects with an established career couldn't be persuaded to join a company that made them reset their PTO to zero. Bissett decided to overhaul the entire package. But because she was new to the company, she had to establish herself before introducing sweeping changes. She started by doing research.

"In Cleveland, we have a great service called Employers Resource Council, which conducts annual surveys regarding company offerings, including PTO and salary," she says. She reviewed competitors' offerings and presented them to upper management. She also gave them insight into the number of employees who were "pointing out." Her findings helped convince management that a change was in order.

Today, all three types of PTO—sick days, personal days, and vacation time—are rolled up into one, which employees, both new hires and current staff, can use as they see fit. The number of hours is prorated, with employees holding one to four years of tenure receiving a total of 128 hours. A rollover policy was also implemented. The end result was an increase in overall employee satisfaction and a major boost in morale—across all ages and company departments. Bissett says that management feels the improved PTO offering was well worth the added cost to the company. "The new system allows employees the freedom to attend their kid's play, take care of a sick parent—whatever they need. It allows them the time to do what they need to get done," she says.

Another area Bissett focused on was working with older workers who were eligible for Medicare but still on Hy-Ko's health benefits. Bissett explained to those workers that Medicare was as good as, if not better than, the health-care options the company offered. Many had been reluctant to make the switch due to what they saw as an intricate system of paperwork, so Bissett helped them with the transition, as well as planned educational seminars and brought in outside specialists to assist with sign-ups and paper processing. "I became somewhat of an expert on Medicare," she says. The program gave employees the chance to see retirement as an option. Of the 10 employees who transitioned to Medicare, 4 retired within the year. "They finally felt comfortable doing so," says Bissett. "Trying out Medicare's offerings before they retired helped alleviate their fears." And those retirees were able to transition slowly out of their responsibilities instead of depart abruptly. It was win-win situation for everyone.

Another benefits area that she's going to change is the 401(k) program. Bissett finds that younger recruits are less interested in a 401(k) package, instead caring more about moving up in the company and achieving better work-life balance. To top it all off, there isn't much incentive to participate because the company doesn't match contributions. Older workers are more excited about this option, but Bissett says, "I believe that if we had a company match, we'd get more people signing up." In her position prior to HY-KO, Bissett says, "we held seminars to explain the 401k plan and exactly what 'pretax dollars' mean. We showed them that if they contributed 30 dollars a week to their 401(k), it only affected their take-home pay by perhaps 10 dollars, because the contribution is based on pretaxed income." The effect was felt immediately: plan enrollment nearly doubled. At Hy-Ko, Bissett says, "we've kind of tweaked our benefits a little bit," and she is planning for even greater changes. "I still think we can be a lot better."

CAREER DEVELOPMENT

Along with the aforementioned benefits changes, Hy-Ko is in the process of implementing its first performance management program. "We used to give cost-of-living or merit increases across the board, usually 3 percent," Bissett explains. "Now everyone has goals and objectives for the year, and you only get an increase if those are met. So you're not going to make the same as your coworker if you don't perform as well as your coworker, and a big part of that, particularly in the plant, is attendance," she says, referring to the aforementioned issue with employees calling in sick.

An added bonus to the program is its appeal to Millennials, who have expressed a desire for more frequent feedback. "It will make a big difference with this group," Bissett says. The more seasoned workers, however, are quite the opposite, often looking to keep their heads down rather than receive recognition. Despite this contrast in desire for acknowledgment, the program will benefit all age groups: Millennials will get their due credit, while all generations will have their career plans clearly mapped out for them, more easily allowing for pay increases and promotions.

Because Hy-Ko already uses several solutions from business outsourcer ADP, tacking on the performance management software came with a relatively small price tag—just a couple thousand dollars. Although the program is too new to analyze its success, the return in morale and productivity will more than compensate for this meager cost, Bissett estimates. For management, the ROI is immense.

SUMMARY

Companies that were established during the time Millennials entered the workforce are more apt to offer packages that are considered progressive, if only because that's the environment the companies were born in. When prospective hires are on the job hunt, it's only natural that they compare offerings between potential places of employment. That means that those companies that still offer old-school packages could be hurting themselves, which is why Hy-Ko has made such a tremendous effort to be more competitive as an employer.

With all of the changes Hy-Ko has introduced, Bissett plans to distribute a survey to get employee feedback. She anticipates a positive response, because she already receives informal glowing reviews. "I get people stopping by my office all the time to say they love the changes," she says. "They want even more." She can also see the difference in the company's turnover rate, which, although it has always been on the low side, has dropped even further.

Despite the challenges in evolving the company, Bissett knows the effort has been worthwhile. "We have a more mature generation here, so that's tough," she admits. New ideas are not always looked upon favorably—whether it be from the enthusiastic younger generations or established company veterans—but Bissett has watched management change its way of thinking to be more open-minded. "We have a long way to go," she says, but she's proud of what has already been accomplished.

CASE STUDY - TECT CORPORATION

Website: www.tectcorp.com

Locations: Based in Fort Mitchell, Kentucky, with other locations in Kansas, Washington, Ohio, California, Georgia, and New York

Founded: 1995

Total employees: 1,300; 25 percent are salaried, 75 percent are hourly, 100 percent within the United States

Employee demographics: 42 percent Traditionalists and Boomers, 37 percent Generation Xers, and 21 percent Millennials

What it does: Aerospace manufacturing

Interviewee: Scott Slocum—Organizational Development Manager

BACKGROUND

With so many of the company's hourly employees nearing retirement age, Slocum recognizes the challenge of preparing for succession planning "before all that knowledge walks out the door." Several leadership and mentoring programs are paving the way for the next generation to step into the roles soon to be vacated by their older peers.

On the positive side, the wide spectrum of ages has made for an inclusive work environment, with engaged employees who go the extra mile to be helpful. Slocum notes that, although in most companies new employees tend to band together, that's not as common at TECT, where bonds are formed more on the basis of personalities rather than company tenure or age group. The diverse staff also makes for a more interesting workplace, he says.

RECRUITMENT

In response to the company's desire to provide a more supportive welcome, Slocum describes the onboarding process TECT has implemented over the past several years: "The first 30 days are scripted for new hires," he says, referring to the meetings that are scheduled with different managers and departments to provide better workplace orientation. A new machine operator or even a freshly graduated engineer might, for example, meet with an employee who's been around for four decades. Slocum mentions an engineering manager who was a co-op student in 1979. "When he sits down for an hour with a kid straight out of college, they start to click right away and generational barriers fall away. That's part of our onboarding process," Slocum says. "It all begins right there" on Day 1.

Although the new onboarding process wasn't wholly driven by studying Millennials, it was one factor. "One thing we learned about this generation is that they're looking for connections right away," Slocum explains. "They really value those relationships, and they're looking for them immediately." As a result of the revamped onboarding process, new-hire retention has jumped from 82 percent to an impressive 90 percent.

COMPANY CULTURE

Whereas once there was reluctance on the part of veteran staffers to work with potential new recruits, today most managers jump at the chance. Slocum describes how this came about through TECT's co-op program, which brings in college students for a few months of practical, hands-on experience. Many of the co-op participants even end up working at the company after graduation.

The company's main partner for the program is the University of Cincinnati, which invented the co-op program back in 1906 and today is still ranked as a leader in the field. When TECT wanted to beef up its program, it started accepting students from the university as young as 19 years old, which caused some managers to vent that they didn't want to "spend their time babysitting." Now, almost five years later, those same managers are practically begging for more co-op participants, having experienced how productive they can be—and even having learned some new tricks from the students, who are learning the latest industry trends in the classroom. This exposure to younger workers has greatly improved interpersonal relations among the company's many generations of employees.

TECT brings in some 40 to 60 co-op students annually from the University of Cincinnati alone, in addition to those recruited through local colleges at the company's other locations. Of the 75 or so salaried employees hired each year, anywhere from three to five come from the company's co-op program.

At times, work style has been a cause of strife at TECT, as it has at many companies, but Slocum has worked through this issue by coaching employees to communicate more with one another. For example, when an employee complains about another leaving before the five o'clock whistle blows, Slocum advises them to talk it out. This has helped improve overall communication and allowed employees to understand that different work styles do not necessarily mean a worker is less productive than one who adheres to more traditional working hours. On a formal level, the company has also provided training on generational differences to their leadership teams. "It's helped them to work through the issues and understand that we're all a little different—and that that's a good thing," says Slocum. Differences bring out the creative side in employees.

CAREER DEVELOPMENT

Although only two years old, TECT's formal mentoring program has already shown results. On their very first day, new hires are given a mentor who has already been through formal training in mentorship. The program not only helps newcomers get oriented but also provides them with someone who can offer continuous career development throughout their time at TECT. "The mentor plays a huge role when it comes to that individual's career path—what they want to accomplish and where they want to go," says Slocum. "The program hasn't been around long enough for us to show ROI, but I already know from what I've observed that it's going to have an impact."

TECT's formal mentoring program has helped bridge the generational gap not only with employees but with customers as well. "A new graduate might have a customer who started working in the '70s," Slocum says, "so you can tap someone on your team who has a similar background for help." Between employees, Slocum has noticed that the mentoring program has allowed older generations to up their tech skills by learning from younger employees.

But the veteran staffers are also picking up new skills on their own, which broke a few misconceptions Slocum himself had about older workers: "Our materials manager in Cleveland, who retired this past fall, started working in 1976. When I arrived at the plant in 2011, I made an assumption about his work style—I thought he'd be a bit archaic. But he surprised me my very first week when I observed him leading the plant and driving us through new implementation on our MRP [material requirements planning] and ERP [enterprise resource planning] systems. He picked that up himself in the middle of his career. So I try not to make those assumptions anymore."

Another one of TECT's programs allows engineers to rotate among departments for a few months each in order to gain exposure to different processes, such as quality and manufacturing. The program, which began just a few years ago, also has employees role-swap, with the newly minted engineers becoming supervisors of the veteran inspectors. "It really helped to break down barriers," Slocum says. "It *forced* it to happen."

Although the first iteration of the program was a little rocky, each successive program has worked out more and more kinks. Slocum relates one story that helped the company rejigger the program:

> We sent a young engineer into a department on the shop floor that has
> a lot of senior employees. His attitude caused the whole thing to go

awry—he was perceived as arrogant and not really into the assignment. But the following year, we tried again, and this time the union president raved about the engineer we sent in. When I asked what was different this time, the employees said it was all in the attitude. The most recent engineer was friendly and eager to learn, which impressed the rest of the team and allowed him to integrate much better than his predecessor. So now we share those learnings with our junior engineers before we send them in. It's made a huge difference.

But the crowning glory of TECT's career development programs is TECT Ed. Now in its fifth year, the initiative nominates roughly a dozen potential leaders from both TECT Power and TECT Aerospace to attend special training for three days, several times a year, at various company location. Originally, the program was only open to degreed employees who had been with the company three or fewer years, but it has since been opened up to include those who have been with the company longer.

Since that change was introduced, Slocum has seen a huge improvement. "I was more pumped up this time around than I've ever been," he says about attending the sessions. "And when I assessed how the sessions had gone, I realized there had been better dialogue and discussion. Veteran employees discussed past procedures, which really enhanced the conversation and gave newcomers something to chew on."

TECT Ed's purpose was to accelerate the learnings that individuals would glean throughout the regular course of their careers, in order to prepare them for leadership sooner. In addition to leadership training, participants get to meet with the CEO and take courses in program management, supply chain management, managing for profit, communications, and Six Sigma, which focuses on process improvement. The program provides a well-rounded overview of the skills and knowledge needed for leadership and career advancement.

Because most of the participants are visiting the company's other locations for the first time, they're exposed to whole new workplace cultures and a new array of faces. "They walk away having a better idea of what their sister plants do," says Slocum." They keep those bonds, and they grow. Their networks just explode. One of the outcomes is we've broken down the walls between TECT Power and TECT Aerospace."

Now that the program, which has already led to innovations and new initiatives between the company locations, has opened its doors to more senior staff, Slocum has noticed additional benefits, such as improved communication among locations and generations. "I could see the stereotypes just breaking down," he observes, before relating a story of how a discussion between two program participants—one older, one more senior—helped bring about a new initiative at the company's Everett plant: "That never would have happened if those two hadn't met, and that happened because of TECT Ed."

Employee retention among program graduates is impressive: 55 of the 70 participants are still with the company. "Participants are the cream of the crop," says

Slocum, "so they're the most susceptible to being recruited by other companies, who also find them attractive. So while we're battling that challenge, it hasn't impacted our enthusiasm for the program."

As at other forward-thinking companies, the implementation of TECT Ed was partially propelled by the desires of Millennials, who Slocum says are interested in companies that show interest in their career growth. "If we don't provide growth opportunities, they won't stay. Millennials are interested in real opportunities to navigate their careers. They may not all aspire to be the CEO, but they have aspirations, and they want to know that their company's going to provide those avenues for them. Successful companies are doing this."

Although Slocum doesn't yet have an ROI on TECT Ed, which he estimates costs $100,000 annually, he cites the nine promotions that have come from recent participants as evidence of its success. "We're feeding the pipeline," he says.

SUMMARY

Enlisting all ages to mentor or fully participate in programs, even those designed for new hires or younger generations, can enhance the experience for all involved, as TECT Ed has proven. Reviewing existing programs and policies to see how they can be made more inclusive can help facilitate conversation, improve interpersonal relationships, and stimulate idea generation.

As for generational assumptions and stereotypes, Slocum offers these words of wisdom: "Stereotypes get in your way and cause you to waste time. After a while, a person's true nature—and value—comes through pretty quickly, but it comes through even quicker if you walk into the situation without those biases."

CASE STUDY - THE ANDERSONS

Website: www.andersonsinc.com

Locations: Based in Maumee, Ohio, with other locations in Alabama, California, Florida, Illinois, Indiana, Iowa, Michigan, Minnesota, Missouri, Nebraska, New York, North Carolina, Ohio, South Carolina, South Dakota, Tennessee, Texas, Utah, Wisconsin. Locations outside the United States include Manitoba (Canada) and Puerto Rico.

Founded: 1947

Total employees: 3,315; 75 percent are salaried, 25 percent are hourly, 0.01 percent are located outside the United States

Employee demographics: 36 percent Traditionalists and Boomers, 30 percent Generation Xers, 34 percent Millennials

What it does: A diversified agribusiness and retailing firm that operates grain elevators, distributes fertilizer, and manages rail cars

Interviewee: Sheri Caldwell—Director, Human Resources, Grain Group

BACKGROUND

An operating group of The Andersons Inc., the Grain Group "provides merchandising and services to the grain industry primarily in the Eastern Corn Belt. We operate over 40 grain elevators in eight states that accept corn, soybean, and wheat commodities and have a total storage capacity of more than 160 million bushels," explains Caldwell, who has been at the company since November 2013. Her division has a wide skill set, thanks to its generationally diverse staff, which ranges from recent college graduates to employees who have been with the company for over four decades. The department taps into this potential by ensuring that all projects and committees comprise the full spectrum of ages.

Caldwell admits that having such diverse age demographics also presents challenges, such as when introducing new technology or processes. The company is currently transitioning to the enterprise software system SAP, for example, and some of the veteran staffers, more so than younger ones, are expressing anxiety about the adjustment. Issues common to other companies, such as differences in work style, are also being addressed. Implementing new programs (including ones inspired by the initiative of a group of younger employees) and a new working environment will further change the landscape, but all for the better, says Caldwell.

COMPANY CULTURE

Differences in communication methods among the generations has had an influence on how the workplace operates. Caldwell has noticed how Millennials prefer to text or use instant messaging systems. "My generation is more e-mail oriented, and the older generations rely more on the phone," she explains. The veteran employees have taken a liking to the Millennials' methods, and it's even helping improve the company's relationships with its customers, who are mainly farmers.

"Older employees want to call or e-mail, while trainees and newer hires instinctively want to text," Caldwell says. "But the communication style really depends on the farmer. It's teaching our employees of all ages to consider how the customer wishes to communicate, not how the employee wants to." And because not all Millennials are as comfortable speaking on the phone as they are sending a text, and Boomers are sometimes befuddled by texting when they first get started, the generations are coaching each other on the best way to communicate using the customer's preferred method.

Other advances influenced by the diversity in generations have sprung up, including an informal group created by Millennials to educate themselves on various industry topics. What started as a low-profile endeavor, with employees sharing articles with one another, quickly became more ambitious, with guest speakers and other employees—including the CEO—speaking about various management and industry issues, including working with the older generations. The HR department took note and decided to formalize a program in order to reach even more of the workforce. "We're developing training on multigenerational interactions in the workplace," Caldwell says.

Because the HR-led program, which came at no cost to the company, is still relatively new, Caldwell said it's difficult to gauge its success just yet, but she did note an improvement in morale due to the increased communication. Some of the original Millennial founders of the information-sharing group manage employees many years their senior, so sharing best practices and anecdotal stories has led to a more collaborative environment. Caldwell hopes the formalized program will continue to boost morale and improve interpersonal relations even further. She also expects to see an increase in productivity. "If employees are hesitant to move forward because they're unsure how to handle a situation or how to communicate with someone, that's inefficient," she explains. "If we address the issue instead, we remove much of that doubt, which allows them to get on with their jobs."

Caldwell has also done one-on-one coaching with veteran employees unaccustomed to the work style of their younger coworkers, who keep untraditional hours but continue working even when outside the office. She explains that a difference in work style doesn't mean an employee is less productive. "It's a foreign concept to some older employees that you can work somewhere other than in the office," she says. And although some at first remain skeptical about this concept, they often come around after conducting a test she suggests: sending a question via e-mail to see how quickly the younger employee replies. More often than not, the experiment ends positively, with the younger employee's quick response easing the veteran's concerns. "It's a culture change," Caldwell explains. "It just takes time and patience with each other."

Caldwell and her HR team also try to promote more community among the generations. "People here love to eat, so we like to throw potlucks," she says. They also hold contests and Super Bowl pools, pitch in for office-wide lottery tickets, and plan other activities that encourage interaction. "When we get everyone involved in something fun, they get to know each other so much better." And that results in better working relationships among the generations.

Modifying existing programs has also been an efficient way to encourage intergenerational interaction. The company already participated in a tutoring program at a local school, so Caldwell simply adjusted how the program was run by pairing younger and older employees as partners. "They have different ways of explaining things to the students," she says. "The students identify with both. They learn from the more seasoned employees' stories of experience, while the younger employees share new insights. And both employees share what they've learned from one another." It's a win-win situation for everyone: the student receives multiple perspectives, and the employees forge a stronger bond with each other.

Caldwell also has several new plans in the works. One of them, a solution for improved employee recognition, she hopes will replace the current outdated system. She describes the new solution as working similarly to Facebook, where any employee can recognize another—whether a superior, a subordinate, or a peer—for an accomplishment, and in some cases even provide a reward such as a gift card, a product, or financial compensation. "It's timely. It's current. People identify with it," she says, acknowledging that many companies are implementing similar systems, due in part to Millennials' desire to receive more frequent acknowledgment for their contributions. And because nearly all employees are now on social media accounts of some sort, many are already accustomed to gamification rewards, such as badges and stickers. Providing a similar experience in the workplace is a natural progression of this trend.

PHYSICAL WORK ENVIRONMENT

One of the bigger changes coming down the pike is a new office building, which will shake up the office hierarchy with its modern layout. In preparation for designing the new blueprint, The Andersons' representatives toured the offices of other companies that went through similar office transformations successfully, to get ideas about what worked—and what didn't. "We asked the other companies what they would change if they could, as well as what they liked about their current spaces," says Caldwell. The research showed a trend in more open environments with fewer individual offices and more collaborative spaces.

Well before the move, many employees—particularly those who would be losing their offices—voiced their concern. Others complained about the lack of formal conference rooms. But Caldwell found that the younger generations were enthusiastic about the change. "I don't get why people are complaining about the lack of privacy," Caldwell cites one younger employee as saying. "I'll just take my laptop and sit in a different spot. Why is it a big deal?" Because younger generations are less concerned with hierarchy, they view the change as a positive.

The new building layout will not only foster better employee interaction, it will also cost far less than if the company had chosen a more traditional layout, because building individual offices is more expensive due to the need for heating and air conditioning plus sprinkler systems. So not only will the new space be more conducive to a progressive work environment, it's also more cost effective than a traditional model. Tearing down the walls—both literally and figuratively—will allow for better communication and increased employee interaction, which is essential when bridging generational gaps.

CAREER DEVELOPMENT

Just as they've influenced how the company's employees communicate, the constantly wired Millennials have also induced change in how The Andersons conducts training. Trainees used to receive enormous binders full of instructional materials to haul with them to a physical classroom, which might not even have been at their location but rather at another office in a different state. "Back then," says Caldwell, "employees would probably rather go to the dentist than sit through a seminar." An upgrade was in order.

Today, the company's employees attend web-based training from their respective locations across the country. And while many of the classes are conducted online, participants are also given real-world assignments, rather than simply told to read case studies from their binders.

With many employees nearing the age of retirement, Caldwell and her team are preparing plans for retaining that knowledge. A newly implemented mentoring program, based on DiSC assessment (a tool used by many companies to identify behavioral differences in employees), partners mentors and mentees based on generations, such as a Boomer paired with a Millennial. The program also seeks to help employees advance more quickly with the help of their veteran mentors.

Caldwell recalls how an older manager gave a younger one a new area of responsibility so that his mentee could gain exposure to a new group. "The older manager told me that he himself had stayed in the same area for too long," she says. "He watched as others passed over him and rose up through the ranks while he stayed in the same position for years." The employee attributed his stagnation to a lack of exposure to other departments and didn't wish for his mentee to experience the same fate. "Take on more," the mentor advised, "and learn new things so you can grow with the company."

While the mentoring program is still in its infancy, Caldwell says she expects it to help the company more easily pass on industry knowledge from veterans to newer employees, while also providing the younger generations with a more transparent system for career development. "It's a really good mix," Caldwell says. "If we didn't have that mixed-age workforce, we wouldn't have such a wealth of knowledge to share with the new hires."

BENEFITS

In order to stay competitive with other employers, the benefits team is looking to change up the company's benefits package. As part of corporate HR's research on the project, the benefits team plan to do a survey to better understand what entices prospective employees, many of whom are part of the Millennial cohort. "We already know that Millennials value freedom and flexibility," she says, referring to the generation's desire for work-life balance, "so maybe they would want to have fewer options for health-care but more for time off."

She knows she might face opposition, recalling a similar change she witnessed while at a previous employer in the health-care industry. A relatively young manager tried to push through a cafeteria-style health-care plan but was opposed by an older manager because "she didn't want to go against what had always been done." The younger manager conducted an informal survey, the results of which convinced the veteran to move forward and announce the changes at an all-hands meeting. The news received a standing ovation from employees.

"The younger employee made her manager look really good, thanks to the research she conducted," Caldwell says, citing this as an example of how others can effect change when confronted with apprehension for something new, which happens often in mature companies with traditional environments. "We knew that many employees might not choose some of the new options, but having the choice improved employee satisfaction."

SUMMARY

New programs or implementations don't need to come with hefty price tags in order for them to be effective. The Andersons was already planning to replace its outdated building, so creating a space that was more progressive and that encouraged employee collaboration, particularly across generations, didn't cost the company extra—it actually saved money. Even programs and activities that are already in place can be used to foster better interaction among the generations. All it takes is a little tweak to a potluck (for example, Boomers bring appetizers, Gen Xers bring main dishes, and Millennials bring dessert) to get the conversation going over courses.

ABOUT THE AUTHOR

Valerie M. Grubb is the principal of Val Grubb & Associates Ltd., which she founded after holding a succession of leadership roles within major corporations, including NBC Universal, Oxygen Media, InterActiveCorp, and Rolls-Royce. She is an innovative and visionary operations leader with an exceptional ability to zero in on the systems, processes, and human capital issues that can hamper a company's growth. Grubb graduated with a mechanical engineering degree from Kettering University and obtained her MBA from the Indiana University Kelley School of Business. She remains highly involved with the Kelley School as a member of the Dean's Advisory Council. She also serves as president of the New York Chapter of Women in Cable Telecommunications and is a board member of the New Orleans Film Society. Valerie recently published a book about her experiences traveling around the world with her mom, entitled *Planes, Canes, and Automobiles: Connecting with Your Aging Parents through Travel* (Greenleaf Book Group, 2015).

INDEX

Note: Page references in *italics* refer to a table.